MEMOIRS
RELATIVE TO
THE STATE
OF
INDIA

MEMOIRS

RELATIVE TO

THE STATE

OF

INDIA

BY

WARREN HASTINGS, ESQ.

GYAN

Published by

GYAN

Gyan Publishing House
5, Ansari Road
Daryaganj, New Delhi-110002
Phone: 011-47034999, 9811692060
E-mail: books@gyanbooks.com

Distribution Network
gyanbooks.com
India, USA, Canada, UK, Australia, France

ISBN: 978-81-212-8218-5 (PB)
First Published, 1786

2nd Impression 2023

Printed at: Gyan Press, Delhi.

MEMOIRS RELATIVE TO THE STATE OF INDIA
Author: WARREN HASTINGS

MEMOIRS

RELATIVE TO

THE STATE

OF

INDIA.

BY

WARREN HASTINGS, Esq.

Late Governor General of Bengal.

A NEW EDITION, WITH ADDITIONS.

LONDON:

PRINTED FOR J. MURRAY, NO. 32, FLEET-STREET.

MDCCLXXXVI.

THE

EDITOR'S PREFACE.

THE following Memoirs were not originally intended for general publication. An imperfect copy having been obtained by Mr. Kearſly, and publiſhed by him, without permiſſion from the author, rendered it neceſſary to give a correct and authentic edition of a work, that has ſo much engaged the attention, and converſation of the world. For this purpoſe Mr. Murray, the preſent publiſher, applied to Mr. Haſtings, and obtained his conſent. The explanatory notes are added by THE EDITOR, and have never been communicated to Mr. Haſtings. Late advices from Bengal enabled the Editor to place ſome ſubjects in a clearer light, and to ſtate as facts what were probabilities only, when Mr. Haſtings reſigned his government. The recovery of a very conſiderable debt from the Nabob Vizier of Oude was ſtated, about two years ago, by very high

 authorities,

authorities, as abſolutely impoſſible; and on a memorable occaſion that debt was not admitted by a late miniſter, in the ſchedule of the property of the Eaſt India Company. When Mr. Haſtings left Bengal, a part of it was paid, and funds appropriated for the complete diſcharge of the remainder in the month of October laſt. It was in that month completely diſcharged, and the Nabob is now in advance to the government of Bengal, for the pay of the Britiſh troops doing duty in his dominions.

In the edition publiſhed by Mr. Kearſly, references are made to papers in an appendix. Theſe references are here omitted. They are in fact totally unneceſſary, as no appendix has been ever publiſhed; and the references in the original publication were left for the advantage of thoſe gentlemen in official ſituations, for whoſe information the firſt copies of this performance were printed. It may be proper, however, to inform the reader, that all the public documents alluded or *referred* to in this work, have already been publiſhed,

published by an order of the House of Commons, in the last session of parliament, and since that period have appeared in various publications.

One curious paper referred to, which has not hitherto been published, the Editor has added in an appendix to this edition. It is a narrative of the flight of the Prince Jehander Shah, eldest son of the Mogul Shah Allum, from his father's court at Dehly. It was written by the Prince in the Persian language, at the request of Mr. Hastings, and translated into English by Captain Jonathan Scott, who has lately published the Memoirs of Eradut Khan.

THE

Author's Advertisement.

THE following ſheets were written at ſea, during my paſſage from India to England. When I began them I had no other deſign than to preſerve and concentrate all the miſcellaneous tranſactions of the three laſt months of my adminiſtration, while they were yet recent in my remembrance.

IN the courſe of this Review, I was imperceptibly led to take in a larger ſcope, as I have ſtated in the work itſelf; and it has acquired ſuch a degree of importance in the judgment of thoſe who have peruſed it, (authorities of which I ſhould ſpeak with the higheſt veneration on any

any occaſion, but one which like the preſent could not but reflect a praiſe on myſelf;) that I have been induced to cauſe a few printed copies to be ſtruck off, for the private information of ſuch perſons as from their official ſituations are intitled to the knowledge which they may be thought to contain.

WARREN HASTINGS.

Bath, Jan. 14, 1786.

ON the 20th of March 1783, I addreſſed a letter to the court of directors, in which I appriſed them of my intention to reſign the ſervice of the Company, leaving a ſufficient interval for the appointment of a ſucceſſor to my office. Had I formed my opinion of the propriety of this intimation on any eſtimate of my own conſequence, the total diſregard which was ſhewn to it might have taught me an humbler leſſon. But in truth, I had ſimply conſidered it as a point of common obligation; and was convinced in my own mind, that the member of the council who ſtood next to me in the regular line of ſucceſſion, was at leaſt as likely to fill the ſtation with ability as any perſon, wanting the ſame local experience, whom the chance of competition might ſubſtitute in his ſtead; for he had been bred and practiſed in the habits of buſineſs, and his manners were conciliating. It would be therefore, at this time, ſuperfluous to aſſign any reaſons for the reſolution which I had taken. Yet theſe were detailed at large in my letter; and if they produced no other effect, they certainly were, as they were intended, a pledge to my firſt conſtituents for the performance of the declaration which I had thus formally made, if no circumſtance intervened which might leſſen the weight of it as an engagement, or which, as a ſuperior claim, might require it to be ſuſpended. In effect, ſuch a contingency did actually come to paſs within a very few months after the date of my letter. This originated in an appeal which was made by the Nabob Vizir and his Miniſters, againſt the acts of Mr. *Briſtow*, the Company's Reſident at his Court, and impelled me, by every tie of juſtice, honour, and public duty, to ſacrifice every conſideration that regarded myſelf alone, if neceſſary, for his redreſs: And that my ſtay for this purpoſe was neceſſary, I may with ſafety at this time affirm, ſince it is demonſtrable, that the purpoſes which were

were the profeſſed objects of my ſtay have been attained, and could not have been attained without it.

I HAD fixed upon the beginning of laſt year for my departure to England. This event determined me to poſtpone it to another ſeaſon; and I may be allowed on ſuch an occaſion to appeal for the evidence, and the ſtrongeſt evidence that could be produced, of the rectitude of my motive, even to an argument of private relation to my own intereſt and feelings, but immediately connected with the reſolution I had taken; ſince it compelled me to ſubmit to a privation of all domeſtic ſociety, and to an expence which muſt be unavoidably repeated whenever I ſhould proſecute the deſign of my own departure to England, and which my fortune could ill afford.

IT was not incumbent upon me to appriſe the Court of Directors formally of this change of my determination, or of the ground of it. Both were obvious. But the original obligation ſtill remained, ſubject to the reſervation of the ſame circumſtances under which it was impoſed.

My return from *Lucnow*, after a long and ſucceſsful application to the re-eſtabliſhment of the affairs of the province of *Oude*, and the due authority of its ruler, replaced me in the ſituation from which I had been drawn by the neceſſity of that attendance. It was, therefore, my firſt care to provide for the execution of the engagement dependant on it, after my arrival.

About the ſame inſtant of time advices were received from England of a bill depending in Parliament for the more effectual regulation of the government of the Britiſh poſſeſſions in India; and as I had deemed it a proper reſpect to the Court of Directors to refer myſelf to their pleaſure for my continuation in the ſervice, if they ſhould think me deſerving of being entruſted with the powers which I had ſtated as neceſſary to enable me to conduct it, I held it proper to wait the reſult of this intelligence, in the poſſibility of its producing that change in the adminiſtration of Bengal, which I had preſcribed as the condition of my ſtay. Of this I adviſed the Court of Directors, in a letter which I wrote to them, dated the 22d of Novemberber, by the Surpriſe; repeating my former declaration, and informing them of my intention to wait the arrival of the next diſpatches which I had been made to expect with the Fox packet, which was waiting at the date of the laſt advices to bring the orders which would be required with the publication of the bill impending.

In the mean time I applied myſelf early and aſſiduouſly to the diſpatch of ſuch arrears of buſineſs as I found depending; and to thoſe exigencies of the government which were likely to preſs, with the ſevereſt weight, upon it, in the event of a change not effected by expreſs authority from home, and therefore wanting the confidence and reſpect of a fixed appointment. The firſt object, and that recently urged by injunctions from the Court of Directors, which rather augmented our difficulties than facilitated the removal of them, was to clear off the debt which we had contracted during the courſe of a long and multiplied war. This conſiſted of two kinds;—Firſt, the regular debt at intereſt, which had continued for ſome time at the fixed ſum of one hundred and ſixty lacks: and Secondly, orders granted on the Treaſury and Depoſits, which at this time amounted to about rupees 144,47,860:8:1. Of theſe orders, ſome, which were in lieu of payment made by the Board of Trade, were charged with the cuſtomary intereſt.

When I left Calcutta at the beginning of the year, I had vainly flattered myſelf, with a confidence which impelled me to expreſs the ſame expectation to the Court of Directors, that we ſhould be able to pay off all the Treaſury orders, and diſcharge a part of the debt at intereſt, by the end of December. I was certainly warranted to form and give this aſſurance by a fair ſtate, which I tranſmitted at the ſame time to the Court of Directors, of our probable receipts and diſburſements to the preſcribed period. The cauſes of my diſappointment aroſe from the unexpected, and equally unneceſſary, detention of Col. *Pearſe*'s detachment at Maſſulipatam, when it was on its return to Bengal; by which an expence of near ſeventeen lacks of rupees was continued a twelvemonth beyond its computed duration; and from the enormous ſum of a crore of rupees, diſtributed

in

in remittances to the other presidencies, of which that of Fort St. George alone, which least wanted it, and of whose disbursements, whatever they were, our Board was kept in utter ignorance, had received for its separate share more than sixty-five lacks. A detail of this subject would be too long an interruption of the general recital; and as it is fully comprised in a letter which was written expressly upon it to the Court of Directors, dated the 6th of December last, and has long since been published.

I was not apprised of these unexpected charges till my return to Calcutta, having trusted to the estimate of receipts and disbursements made at the beginning of the year above quoted, as a sure provision against them. I was anxious to put an immediate check to the continuance of a drain which our finances could ill sustain, and happily found the other members of the Board in the same disposition and opinion. At our first meeting in council on the 8th of November, I proposed, and it was agreed to with such a promptneſs that our orders were written and ſigned before we parted, to ſend a peremptory injunction to the preſidency of Fort St. George, to deſiſt from further drafts upon us, declaring that we would anſwer none that were granted after the receipt of our letter.

To Bombay, whoſe wants were more preſſing, but had already received a very ample and acknowledged relief, we wrote to confine their demands within five lacks of rupees, until they ſhould receive our licence for a larger ſupply; and to this we afterwards added the promiſe of a further remittance, by bills from the treaſury of Lucnow in the month of May next; for which a proviſion had been expreſsly made on a very profitable rate of exchange in the Kiſtbundy, or account of inſtalments, agreed upon by the Nabob Vizir in payment of his debt to the company.

A FEW days before my return to Calcutta, but while I remained at a ſmall diſtance from it, a packet was received from the Court of Directors, which had been diſpatched by land, and contained a letter dated

dated the 15th of June; in which they severely cenſured the Governor General and Council, for having agreed, in the month of November 1784, to take up the ſum of fifty lacks, on loan for draughts on the Court of Directors, to ſupply a deficiency of nearly that amount in the advances made for the inveſtment of the year; when, as it appeared to them, our former advances had greatly exceeded the value of the allotted proviſion; and they therefore recommended to the Board to prevail upon the ſubſcribers to accept of a redemption of their loans in lieu of the promiſed bills.

As this diſpatch had been made for the ſole and expreſs purpoſe of conveying the ſentiments and orders of the Court of Directors on that ſingle ſubject; and therefore ſtrongly manifeſted the impreſſion which it had made on their minds, and impreſſed the conſequent neceſſity of compliance on ours; the part which we had to chooſe was both difficult and hazardous. The order was evidently founded on a miſtake; for the Court of Directors, or rather, as we muſt ſuppoſe, their official reporter, had confounded the advances of two years with thoſe of one. It was a becoming deference to conclude that, as the propriety of the order was inſeparably connected with the truth of the fact to which it was applied, they would not have paſſed the order under a contrary ſuppoſition; and that a diſcovery of the error would induce them to revoke it.

OUR engagements had hitherto been held moſt ſacred, the Court of Directors having contented themſelves with expreſſing their diſapprobation of ſuch as they deemed not ſufficiently warranted; but never diſputing their validity, or withholding their effect, if it depended on them for giving it; and the former loans, which had been contracted on the ſame conditions, and for the ſame exigency, had received their expreſs approval in terms of applauſe. To receive their recommendation in the conſtruction of an abſolute order, and to execute it literally as ſuch, under the circumſtances which have been recited, would have been injurious to the ſervice, highly culpable in its principle, productive of much aggravated diſtreſs in its immediate operation, and deſtructive of our future credit; fatally, perhaps, to the Company's pany's exiſtence, if ever a ſeaſon ſhould recur of the like difficulties with thoſe which our credit had hitherto enabled us to ſurmount: at the ſame time to perſiſt in a literal adherence to our engagements with the knowledge of ſuch an indiſpoſition in the Court of Directors towards them, would have been an injury to the ſubſcribers, if the Court ſhould refuſe to ratify them. Upon the whole, after much diſcuſſion, but little debate, a middle expedient was adopted; which was, to publiſh the whole ſtate of the caſe, and to give the ſubſcribers an option, either of the redemption of their loans, or of the acceptance of their bills, and to refer the latter to the juſtice and candour of the Court of Directors for their ratification of them. This ſubject engaged much of the attention of the Board in their two firſt meetings, held on the 8th and 9th of November, and paſſed with their unanimous aſſent. The inſtant effect was ſuch as could not fail to afford us the moſt complete ſatisfaction; for the publication made no alteration in the minds of the ſubſcribers, who retained their original intereſt in the ſubſcription, only 2,51,500 rupees of it having been withdrawn, principally by perſons

persons acting as trustees for others, and therefore not choosing to exercise the same latitude of judgment with those whose property was at their own disposal.

I FOUND the Board engaged in an unpleasant altercation with the Board of Trade, which had originated from prior orders of the Court of Directors, received by the Surprise Packet, which had left England on the 29th of April, and arrived in Calcutta on the 28th of August. These contained some severe censures upon the Board of Trade for a latitude assumed in their allotment of contracts for the provision of the investment, and a peremptory injunction to grant them, after due advertisement, to the best bidder. Our Council, in implicit submission to the letter of the order, exacted from the Board of Trade an immediate obedience to it; to which the Board of Trade objected, pleading, that in consequence of an intimation given them by the Superior Council, early in the year, of their intention to appropriate one complete crore of rupees for the service of the investment of the season, not accompanied or followed by any other instructions,

instructions, they had issued immediate orders to their former agents and contractors, that no time might be lost for so large a provision, to continue their advances on the terms of the last year; that these orders were intended and received as actual engagements, though not confirmed by any formal deeds, and had certainly the same effect after so long a lapse of time; that the season for making the advances, and other preparatory acts, was long since passed, and the season for the returns approaching; and that any attempt to cancel the existing engagements, against which they thought the contractors would have their remedy at law, and to transfer them to new adventurers, with the necessary time allowed for public notice, and for possession, would occasion a total loss of the investment for the season.

To these objections, which really possessed all the weight given to them by the Board of Trade, it might have been added, that the order of the Court of Directors, though, as I recollect, rather indefinitely worded, must have been intended for a rule of general practice, and could not

not poſſibly be meant for immediate application; ſince it would not have been received till the latter end of October, or the beginning of November, if the Surpriſe had made her paſſage in the ordinary time, which ſhe had ſhortened by two months; and of courſe the Board of Trade would have been in the receipt of part of the goods provided, and the reſt would have been in the courſe of delivery. At all events, the order was now become ineffectual. It was therefore propoſed, and happily agreed to, to cloſe the conteſt, by yielding the point of it to the Board of Trade, and allowing their engagements to ſtand with the reſponſibility thrown on them for its effect with relation to the orders received from home. At the ſame time, as the Court of Directors in their report delivered to the Houſe of Commons on the 23d of March 1784, and which they had called upon us with much ſolemnity to verify, had ſtated the whole ſum of the expected cargoes from India for that year at one million ſterling, of which the proportion that Bengal alone bore to the other preſidencies was but thirty lacks; the Board of Trade was required to limit the

the provision to that sum for the prescribed articles of their investment, with the addition of fifteen lacks for raw silk, which was not in the list; both to allow for the provision actually made, and to preserve the manufacture, which had been much improved both in price and quality. The Board of Trade contended for a larger allowance; but a peremptory declaration of the Superior Board prevented a repetition of the demand.

I have said, that it was the first object of the Board (it was at least my own) to clear off our debts, by lessening our disbursements, as the only means of fulfilling the commands and expectations of the Court of Directors, and of affording an effectual relief to the other presidencies; since a lavish dissipation of our treasures beyond our current income, however specious the occasion might appear, or however urgent the call might be, as it was in the instance of the orders of the Court of Directors, grounded on their report presented to the House of Commons, would only add to our difficulties, not unlike a thread drawn to its utmoſt length from an entangled ſkain. Our natural exigencies muſt be ſupplied; the army muſt be paid a portion of its arrears for its ſubſiſtence, and the larger was their amount the leſs would it admit of increaſe; the whole amount, therefore, of the annual pay, of whatever denomination, muſt after a certain run be diſtributed to them: the reſtoration of peace, and the return of our foreign detachments, required that as large a portion of the army ſhould be diſbanded as had been ſuperadded to our fixed eſtabliſhment in the courſe of the war; but the corps which were to be diſbanded, were to be firſt paid up to the period of their ſervice; nor could they be paid, and the others neglected, without exciting general diſcontent, at all times dangerous in tranſactions of military œconomy; but above all, when the neceſſity of retrenchments, and the known intention of making reformations, had diſpoſed the minds of men to a quicker reception of ſuch impreſſions as led to mutiny: expedients, if they were to be found, muſt be uſed, either to anſwer or to ſhift the

actual

actual demand; and every such expedient will be found to be the present gain of one rupee for the future loss of two: the debt as it increased, would throw the prospect of payment to a greater distance, and proportionably increase the discount of the original sums, which was already very large both on the Interest Notes and Treasury Orders: the multitude of bills unpaid created the like accumulation of accounts unaudited, and the consequent licentiousness of contingent charges, besides the natural incitement to irregular claims when the expected receipts were either partial or remote. Though the Treasury was ostensibly charged with the established rate of interest, its substantial loss was equal in most cases to the discount, since every contractor, and other dealer on trust, either with the Board, or Board of Trade, took the difference into the account, either by enhancing the rates of originating engagements, or eluding the conditions of the old. Yet the debt itself was inconsiderable: and here it may not be amiss to take notice of the fallacy of the general cry which has prevailed for some time past, of the loss of our publick credit; than which nothing can be more foreign from the truth.

THE fact is, that our publick credit, by which I mean the credit of our Interest Notes, and Treasury Orders, never extended beyond the English servants of the Company, and the European inhabitants of Calcutta; and to these may be added a few, and a very few, of the old Hindoo families at the presidency. All the other inhabitants of the provinces are utterly ignorant of the advantage and security of our funds, and have other ways of employing their money, such as purchases of landed property, loans at an usurious and accumulating monthly interest, and mortgages; to which, though less profitable in the end, and generally insecure, they are so much attached by long usage, and the illusion of a large growing profit, that it would not be easy to wean them from these habits for others more difficult of comprehension, and to them of insuperable discredit from the idea of insecurity, attached to the dependance on power. And happy for the Company is it, that such bounds are prescribed by necessity to their

their public credit; and that it is not in the power of a weak adminiſtration to load its ſucceſſors with debts improvidently contracted for the relief of its own exigencies.

THE want of credit, as it is falſely called, in Bengal, is not, as the term implies, a want of confidence, but of means, in thoſe who were the creditors of our treaſury. When theſe had no more ready money to lend, the government appeared to be greatly diſtreſſed, becauſe its expences continued at the ſame amount with the reſource ſtopped, by which they had been ſupplied beyond the extent of its current income; and as the proſpect of diſcharging the debt which it had contracted, became ſo much the more remote, and in a degree doubtful from the hazards of a ſtate of multiplied warfare, its notes firſt loſt their equal currency by a natural conſequence, and afterwards ſunk yet more in their value. The ſame cauſes afterwards affected the orders on the Treaſury, although in the courſe of payment, but at uncertain periods. Yet, when I left Bengal, our debts of every denomination amounted to no more than 304,00,000 current rupees, which is little more than one-half of our annual revenue, which may be fairly eſtimated at 5½ crores of current rupees, or 5½ millions ſterling.

WITH this clear, and certainly true ſtate of the queſtion, how will it appear to any candid judgment, that after a war ſuſtained during the courſe of five years with three States of the greateſt relative power to our own ſituation and connections, the Marattahs, Hyder Ally Cawn, and the French; after having ſent two great armies to the extremities of Indoſtan and Deccan; after having furniſhed ſubſiſtence to the other preſidencies, ſupplied the China Trade with yearly remittances, and made richer inveſtments for England than were ever purchaſed in the ſame ſpace of time under any preceding adminiſtration; our reſources are exhauſted, and our credit gone, becauſe we owe a ſum which we cannot inſtantly diſcharge, but *which ſcarcely exceeds half our annual revenue!* I repeat the poſition in the ſame terms, be-

cauſe

caufe it cannot be too often repeated, nor its impreffion too forcibly made in fuch a difcuffion. Let the fame cafe be put of a private eftate fo encumbered, and its proprietor reduced by it to a ftate of bankruptcy. It is an abfurdity in terms:—but if the comparifon be carried higher to the enormous magnitude of the fum in which the parent ftate is indebted, a fum which all the treafures of this habitable world could not realize, the attempt to fix the imputation of infolvency on the treafury of Bengal would be too contemptible for argument *.

When I took charge of the government of Bengal in April 1772, I found it loaded with a debt at intereft of nearly the fame amount as the prefent; and in lefs than two years I faw that debt completely difcharged, and a fum in ready cafh of the fame amount actually accumulated in ftore in the public Treafuries; and in effect the prefent debt ought to be cleared off, as I

* The debts of every denomination, contracted in Bengal during the late fuccefsful war in India, fcarcely exceeded three millions fterling. The unfunded debt alone of Great Britain was, two years after the peace, thirty-fix millions.

have no doubt it will be, completely, in two years of peace, if the preſent peace is of that duration.

SOME time before my departure the Accomptant General delivered in to the Board an eſtimate of the probable reſources and diſburſements of the Bengal government from the 30th of April 1784 to the 1ſt of May 1785; from which it appeared, that at the end of that period the claims on our Treaſury would exceed our reſources by 1,49,01,433 current rupees: or, in other words, that independantly of our bonds we ſhould be indebted this ſum, either for loans, or for arrears of pay, or other current diſburſements. On the ſuppoſition that this ſtatement were juſt, this would be a heavy debt or deficiency. But even this, which I deem exaggerated, will be found, on a comparative examination, to be conſiderably leſs than what actually exiſted at the time when the account was formed. For the proof of this aſſertion, I refer to the account itſelf, No. in the Appendix. From thence it appears, that on the 30th of April, 1784, we were indebted as follows;—

Balance

Balance due to ſundry departments.		2,87,146.12:11
Diſburſements in arrears, viz.		
Civil	16,55,934:6	
Military	51,38,887:13:5	
Marine	3,39,486:15:1	
Revenue department	17,77,126: 6:7	
		89,11,435: 3: 7
Extraordinary diſburſements in arrears, viz.		
For depoſits due from the Treaſury	10,47,600:13: 2	
Due on ſundry orders thereon	2,87,142:11: 5	
Due on ditto in favour of the Board of Trade	45,45,897: 5: 7	
Due on ditto for ſurplus to, and drafts of the other preſidencies.	24,39,750: 3	
Due from the *Lucknow* Treaſury to the Bankers and Mr. *Scott*	18,21,707: 8: 8	
Due on various accounts	63,886:13:10	
		102,05,985:7:8
Current Rupees		1,94,04,567:8:2

THE amount therefore of our debt and arrears, independent of Bonds, on the 30th of April 1784, was 1,94,04,567:8:2 current rupees; but from this we ſhould in juſtice deduct the amount of the ſums remaining at the ſame period in charge of the different offices, being 40,63,877:2:6 current rupees: and the real deficiency of our finances at that time will be found 1,53,40,690:5:8 current rupees, being more than the deficiency calculated for the 1ſt of May, 1785, by 4,39,256:9:9 current rupees.

MANY of the articles which compoſed our debt in April 1784, would run on without much inconveniency to the creditors till May 1785; and there are ſome even which could not with propriety be diſcharged. Of the former kind, are the orders on the Treaſury, of which as ſome were paid off, others might be granted to an equal amount.

SUCH alſo are the arrears of ſome of the offices. Of the latter kind are the depoſits in the Treaſury, which are never reſtored until demanded, and which have continued for a long ſeries of years at nearly the ſame amount.

BUT

But in fact, this estimate, though formed with all possible accuracy at the time, has from changes of circumstances, in the intervening period, already proved in many particulars erroneous; the receipts being under-rated, and the disbursements stated beyond their real amount. I will mention a few instances.

The sales of the Salt are rated in this account for the whole year at only thirty lacks of rupees; whereas, it appears from an actual account delivered to me by the Controller, that on the 31st of December 1784, he had paid into the Treasury, 44,20,000 sicca rupees; and he expected to make further payments by the 30th of April 1785, to the amount of nine lacks, making altogether 53,20,000 sicca rupees, 61,71,200 current rupees; and the event has hitherto always more than verified the amount of his estimates.

The receipts from the Opium are in the same manner estimated under their probable amount, having already been exceeded by the proceeds arising from only a part of the Opium, which was sold a few

few days before I left Calcutta. The whole ſales, when completed, would yield about ſeventeen lacks, being five lacks more than Mr. *Larkins* has ſtated in his account.

I DO not ſee any eſtimate in this account of the receipts ariſing from the ſales of the Company's Europe imports; theſe may be computed on a medium at nine lacks.

THE grounds on which I ſuppoſe that Mr. *Larkins* has ſtated the diſburſements at a higher rate than they will actually amount to, are theſe: the eſtimate is calculated at the rate of our eſtabliſhments in April 1784; but in the month of January 1785, a general reduction took place in all our eſtabliſhments, both civil and military, which would have a conſiderable effect in diminiſhing the diſburſements of the three remaining months of the year. As this reduction extended generally to the eſtabliſhments dependant on the various offices which were aboliſhed, without particularizing each article; the exact amount of the whole ſaving cannot be aſcertained, until the

the particular accounts formed in conſequence of it are received from Bengal. Setting aſide the effects of this reduction, if the circumſtances which I have before-mentioned are taken into the eſtimate, the ſtate of our deficiency may be corrected as follows :—

Deficiency per Mr. *Larkins'* eſtimate on the 30th of April 1785, viz.			1,49,01,433:11:11
Deduct receipts beyond what Mr. *Larkins* has eſtimated, viz.			
Further receipts from the Salt	23,00,000		
Ditto the Opium	5,00,000		
Receipts from the import ſales ——	9,00,000		
Sicca Rupees	37,00,000		
Batta 16 per cent.	5,92,000		
		42,92,000	
Total deficiency eſtimated for the 1ſt of May 1785			1,06,09,433:11:11

Which is leſs than what I have ſhewn was our deficiency on the 30th of April 1784, by 47,31,256:9:9 current rupees.

I NOW proceed. As almoſt every act of the Board which was not in the ordinary courſe of buſineſs, during the ſhort interval comprehended in this review was formed on the principle which I have already

ready mentioned, or with a view to it; I ſhall recite them as they accord with the general ſubject, leaving ſuch as are of a different kind to follow without regard to the order of time in which they paſſed.

In the conſultation of the 22d of November, two other reſolutions paſſed, which afforded the proſpect of conſiderable relief in our means of expence: One, to withold the ſupply to Canton, which was the leſs neceſſary, as the ſupercargoes, who beſt knew their own wants, had not required it; and we knew that they could generally command any ſum that they might have occaſion for, by drafts on the Court of Directors. The other was immediately connected with it. The uſual mode of remittance to Canton was by opium, either ſent on account of the Company, or by ſale to individuals, the amount of the ſales being payable to the Company's caſh in China.

By the firſt we were conſtantly loſers, and I believe ſuch will be the invariable conſequence of attempts of the Superior Adminiſtration, charged as it is with ſo great a variety of affairs, to entangle itſelf

in

in the nice and intricate minutiæ of commerce; and in the latter the opium had always ſold below its real value, or, to ſpeak more properly, below the value which the firſt ſale ought to bear in the proportion of its demand, and eaſy ſale abroad.

It was agreed to advertiſe the ſale of it in lots at public auction, and to receive Treaſury Orders in payment. By this advantage fairly taken of the eagerneſs of individuals to convert their Treaſury Orders into caſh, or uſeful merchandiſe, we cleared off more than ſixteen lacks of our current debt, and raiſed the ſale of the opium to a profit exceeding by much the diſcount of our Treaſury Orders.

At this time we had more ſhips on hand, reckoning thoſe which were expected, than we could provide with cargoes. Our ſupplies to Bombay, though very ample, were yet inſufficient for all their wants. Their inveſtments of coffee we underſtood to be an eſſential article; in ſo much, that in the laſt year they had ſent one of the Company's ſhips to Mocha for

for a cargo of coffee in the expectation of obtaining it on credit, but failed; and the ship returning empty, they purchased at an advance of fifty per cent. on the prime cost, and drew upon Bengal for the amount, a quantity sufficient for her lading, from a private adventurer. This may serve for one illustration of the improvidence of desultory expedients. It occurred to us that one of the ships which was then laying in the river might be profitably employed in this service, and the Camden was accordingly chosen for it. The Board of Trade was directed to provide for the purpose a small investment of cloth and rice, the produce of which was to be invested in coffee, with an allowance to the commander to draw upon the Company for the deficiency.

I AM aware that it will perhaps be objected to some of these measures, that in relieving our own exigencies we have only increased the burthen of the Company, by leaving it to fall on them with accumulated weight from other parts of their general administration; that for instance, in stopping the supplies to China we have entailed

entailed on the Company the expence of paying the bills which the ſupercargoes muſt draw for money taken up at Canton; or, that in prohibiting further drafts from Madraſs, we have obliged that preſidency to reduce their inveſtment, or to borrow money at a large intereſt, or, in more propriety of ſpeech, to iſſue bonds in lieu of payment for their current expences.

Such objections, though they are in reality inapplicable, yet being mixed with facts, to thoſe who conſider the ſubject ſuperficially, will appear juſt, and more eſpecially where the mind is already prepoſſeſſed with thoſe ideas which have been ſo univerſally adopted, and which, in truth, have been one great cauſe of our preſent embarraſſments.

It ſeems to have been ſuppoſed that the reſources of Bengal were inexhauſtible; and to the meaſures which ſprung from ſuch ideas muſt we aſcribe a great part of the diſtreſs which its government has experienced.

Whatever

WHATEVER charges might be incurred at the other presidencies, whether occasioned by speculative plans of encreasing their investment, or by a lavish waste of their treasure, it was the less regarded how far their own resources fell short of their disbursements, since Bengal was looked on as an inexhaustible fund from whence the deficiency might easily and readily be supplied. Hence it is, that the drains from Bengal for the support of the other presidencies have been annually increasing, till at length they have amounted in 1784, as I have already observed, to the enormous sum of a crore of rupees.

IT is true that the resources of Bengal are great; but they are not inexhaustible. After defraying all the charges of its government, and all expences of its civil and military establishments, Bengal is perhaps capable of yielding an annual tribute of one crore of rupees to the Company; nor is it material to the country whether the remittance be made entire in cargoes exported to England, or divided by aids sent to the other presidencies and China; but it can only be made through the medium of trade. Every rupee drawn from its currency, whether in ſpecie or in bills, which will amount to the ſame effect in the end, will gradually exhauſt it of its vital ſtrength; nor will the effect be felt until it will be too late to adminiſter a remedy for it. The ſources of opulence which it poſſeſſes in the fertility of its ſoil, and the number and induſtry of its inhabitants, will, I think, admit of its yielding the tribute I have mentioned; which is perhaps greater than any other country in the world could bear, poſſeſſed only of the ſame ſources, and like it, without any mines of gold or ſilver. But if more is to be improvidently exacted, theſe ſources may fail, and Bengal be rendered incapable of yielding what it might have done with eaſe. The ordinary ſupplies to the other Preſidencies, which were once moderate, were ſufficient for their wants; ſuch may not now be adequate to the effectual relief of their preſent exigencies; yet it is certainly better, that the means of furniſhing them in future ſhould be preſerved, than that by attempting too much, they ſhould be cut off for ever. Bengal wants only a little reſpite to retrieve its own affairs. It will then with eaſe furniſh the uſual ſupplies to the other Preſidencies, and perhaps be able to increaſe them, ſo as to aſſiſt in clearing off their incumbrances. But if the ſtrain be carried too far on Bengal in its preſent ſtate, I predict, that not only its capacity of aſſiſting the others muſt annually diminiſh, but its own embarraſſments increaſe ſo as to endanger its very exiſtence, if ever it ſhould be preſſed by any calamity. The recovery of Bengal is the object therefore of the firſt conſequence to the Company, and is in effect the firſt mode of ſubſtantial relief to the other Preſidencies.

Of the two foreign detachments, one had been ſome time returned from Surat, under the conduct of Colonel Charles Morgan, and diſſolved. The other, commanded by Colonel Pearce in the Carnatic, had been unfortunately detained at Maſſulepatam, as I have before obſerved, during the laſt ſeaſon preceding the rains, and did not repaſs the boundary of Bengal till the end of the laſt year. I ſtaid long enough

enough for the melancholy pleaſure of ſeeing the remains of this valuable corps after its return, and to join in the regretful, but neceſſary order for its diſſolution. Theſe reductions, by the abolition of an expenſive ſtaff, and a heavy contingent expence, will prove a conſiderable relief to our general military charge. But a more extenſive and radical cure was yet wanted for the great diſeaſe of our finances, and this I had the inexpreſſible ſatisfaction to ſee completed, and adminiſtered before my departure. One plan was formed for a general retrenchment of all the civil, and another of all the military eſtabliſhments. Theſe appeared before the Board in their firſt and rough ſtate on the 20th of December, and were paſſed on the 4th of January.

AMONG the many invectives, whether excited by policy, malevolence, or truth, which have been thrown upon the adminiſtration of Bengal, that of a laviſh expenditure of the public money, in current expences and in fixed eſtabliſhments, has been a conſtant and laboured ſubject of declamation. Allufions are made to it as to a fact of fuch notoriety, as to preclude the neceffity of evidence; at leaft, no inftances have been adduced in proof of it, which have come to my knowledge. No credit has been given to the government of Bengal for having added more than a crore of rupees *, in the midft of all its difficulties, to the public revenue; no remembrance retained of the applaufe beftowed on the fame adminiftration for former retrenchments made, and a fyftem of œconomy formed, when the temper of the times admitted it; no confideration allowed for the fums invefted in the fupport of the Company's commerce, which it has alone fupported; nor for the defence of the Company's other Prefidencies, which but for that defence would have been loft; no merit afcribed to it for having maintained the fplendor of the national character in all its military operations, unalloyed by a fingle failure of fuccefs, or imputed error; nor for having infured the bleffings of peace, fecurity, and abun-

* One million, one hundred thoufand pounds fterling.

dance

dance, to the ſubjects of its immediate dominion, while it dealt out the terrors of conqueſt to the remoteſt enemies of the parent ſtate, and of its own aſſociate members; and while every other member of the Britiſh Empire was afflicted with the plagues of war or inſurrection. As little was it noticed, with how inconſiderable a charge upon its fixed reſources theſe ſervices were performed, and how diſproportionate, beyond all degrees of compariſon, with the growth of the national debt, or with the product of that debt in the national ſervices, within the ſame period. It was ſufficient that our expences had greatly exceeded thoſe of our peace eſtabliſhment, to infer from it, without further enquiry, that the exceſs was ſolely the effect of diſſipation.

YET let me be allowed to repeat the ſuppoſition which I have already taken occaſion to make: were Lord *Clive* to awake from the dead, or Mr. *Vanſittart*, great as was the mind of the former, and extenſive as the knowledge, and ready the reſources of the latter, and to be told what powerful exertions had been made by Bengal within the laſt ſix or ſeven years, and what was its actual ſtate and capacity; neither one nor the other would give credit to the information, but pronounce it to be impoſſible from the recollection of what they knew of the powers of that Government, and from any allowance which they could make for its ſubſequent improvements.

YET I do not affirm that the charge was abſolutely groundleſs. There never yet was a ſyſtem of public œconomy to which it would not in a degree apply. Some of its offices were overpaid, nor were the emoluments allotted to all exactly proportioned to their importance, truſt, or the ability required for diſcharging them. It is impoſſible that they ſhould, where offices exiſt at the time in which their ſalaries are determined, and many are to determine them. Men were not invariably appointed to offices to which they were ſuited, or beſt ſuited by their talents, experience, or integrity. It is impoſſible that they ſhould, where the power of patronage is in many hands, and exerciſed under

under the influence of perſonal favour, or of ſuperior patronage.

CONTINGENT bills, which form the moſt uncontroulable ſource of the general diſburſements, were neither audited as they came in, (and every delay is in this caſe a cauſe of increaſe in expence) nor when audited, corrected with that ſeverity with which contingent accounts ought to be corrected; and the foregoing cauſes may be alledged for this effect alſo.

TO enumerate every caſe would be endleſs. In a word, while the power of Government is in the hands of many; and the ſmaller the number is, the greater is the evil in this caſe; while each hand holds an equal ſhare of it; while the members of government retain their places by ſufferance, and the terrors of diſmiſſion and diſgrace are held out againſt them at home; when their accuſers and the expectants of their places are the judges of their conduct, and preparers of the evidence on which it is to be tried; when the members of the government themſelves are in diſagreement with each other, and that diſagreement (with regret and ſhame I ſuppoſe it) is excited by the voice of authority; when each member ſtands in need of ſupport from home, and owes returns for the ſupport which he receives; when each claims an indulgence from the others, and has it in his power to retaliate every diſappointment, which may be eaſily underſtood, but can never be imputed; and laſtly, when the moſt meritorious conduct is denied its credit, and even the ſacrifices of intereſt are branded with the reproach of venality; from a government ſo conſtituted, what reformation can be expected?

YET what could be done, has been done; and I know not whether I feel moſt ſatisfaction or regret in the reflection, that my adminiſtration cloſed with an act which though moſt neceſſary to the public expectation, will give cauſe of mortal offence to numbers both in India and in England, and ſubject me to the charge of ingratitude from every friend at home who regards the return of perſonal favour as an obligation

obligation ſuperior to the conſideration of public exigency; and I expect to experience this, and worſe effects of it. Yet there never was a time in which I ſtood in more need of perſonal ſupport, or had a ſtronger private inducement to court it. But as I ſaw a neceſſity for attempting a new and complete reformation, I could not reconcile it with duty or honour, to leave ſo invidious a work to my colleagues, when I could render it leſs odious, to them at leaſt, by taking a ſhare, and a principal one, in the formation of it; when I thought (as every man in my ſtation ought to think) that I could perform it with more effect than others could; and eſpecially when I conſidered, that it was an act that would, or ought at leaſt, to extend in its operation to the diſtance of years beyond my own time, and was therefore the moſt important ſubject of my attention, as the moſt laudable of my ambition. As to the execution, that is the moſt eaſy part of it; for when the plans are formed and iſſued in orders, what remains is merely negative: and it will require little trouble to refrain from creat-

ing

ing new offices, or additions of ſalary; nor ſtretch of capacity to refuſe unneceſſary advances of caſh, or the ſanction of prohibited charges.

Before I left Calcutta on my viſit to Lucnow, in February 1784, I with ſome difficulty prevailed on the Board to conſtitute a committee for auditing accounts. I was induced to recommend this meaſure, by the long experience of the inſufficiency of the ſuperior Board for that kind of detail, eſpecially where the members of it did not mutually poſſeſs an implicit confidence, and moſt cordial agreement. Beſides, the examination of accounts requires an ocular inſpection, and that kind of abſtracted attention whieh cannot be beſtowed on a Secretary reading them, nor by many ears attending. In effect, though the Board aſſembled regularly on every Thurſday in their department of inſpection, for the profeſſed purpoſe of examining accounts; I can ſecurely affirm, that the whole aggregate of buſineſs tranſacted by the Board in this department collectively, in the courſe of a twelvemonth, was

not

not equal to that which a ſingle member, uninterrupted, could have diſcharged in one morning.

In the plan which I gave in for the formation of the new office, and which was paſſed with little alteration, I adopted the conſtruction of the Board of Accounts which exiſted at Fort St. George at the time in which I was a member of the Council there; and which was admirably calculated for quick diſpatch, as well as to preclude, as much as poſſible, all unfairneſs from prejudice or favour.

I was the more deſirous of effecting this point at the time, from the apprehenſion of being long abſent from the Preſidency; and I flattered myſelf that by this expedient the moſt important and eſſential part of the current buſineſs would be diſpatched with regularity. The event did not anſwer my expectations, the conſtruction of the Committee differing eſſentially from the principles of its conſtitution. The civil audits were indeed brought up to the lateſt period, which was a very material point attained; but the military, the moſt important, were in long arrears, and the accounts of all the foreign detachments, which the Board had with great labour examined, and either paſſed the minuter corrections, or laid down the general rules for thoſe which were of the ſame kind, but of more frequent occurrence, with orders for their reference for complete adjuſtment to the Commiſſary General, remained after the lapſe of a year unnoticed, having neither been tranſmitted to the Commiſſary General, nor even tranſcribed from the rough minutes. Theſe, and all the other depending accounts, underwent the ſeparate inſpection of the members of the Board, a work of great labour; thoſe of the military detachments referred with proper inſtructions to the Commiſſary General, and all the reſt brought up to the end of the month of December, by the 27th of the month enſuing.

I HAVE enlarged on this ſubject beyond the claim which it may appear to have from its obvious conſequence; both becauſe caufe it is connected with the general principle of frugal œconomy, and with the principle of that duty with which I fhall clofe this recapitulation; I mean the obligation of leaving as few incumbrances as poffible on the hands of my colleagues, and efpecially of my fucceffor; and for that purpofe of beftowing an unufual portion of my own perfonal labour upon them before my departure.

In my accommodation with the Nabob *Affoph ul Dowlah*, I had agreed to withdraw the detachment commanded by Col. Sir *John Cumings*, from Furruckabad, and had continued the eftimate of its expence in the fum which the Nabob was charged with for the current year no longer than to the end of December, allowing the intermediate time for the return of the detachment within our own borders; and I left orders for that effect in the hands of my military fecretary Major *Palmer*, whom I left as my agent at Lucnow, to be iffued whenever the force deftined to fupply its place from the Nabob's own eftablifhment fhould be ready to occupy the ftation. This

This detachment ſtood at a yearly charge of near twenty-three lacks of rupees, of which nine lacks conſiſted in ſtaff-allowances, and excluſive diſburſements appertaining to it as a ſeparate corps. The laſt ſum would have been immediately ſaved by the reduction; and a ſaving of the whole, or nearly the whole, might have followed by the diſcharge of as many ſepoy regiments as the number compoſing the detachment, no longer wanted with the termination of the ſervice in which it was then employed. I had once before attempted the ſame meaſure in the year 1782, and had even recalled the detachment then ſtationed at Furrackabad; but I was under a neceſſity, cauſed by many conſiderations of a policy to which I ſhould have yielded little reſpect under a better conſtituted ſyſtem of government, to revoke it. The Nabob had never ſolicited the aid of a military force for the defence of that frontier, and he alone was, or ought to be, the judge of his own wants. In truth, it was not wanted; but it greatly injured his authority, it affected his revenue, and added a large ſum to the annual

nual exceſs of his debt to the Company, without any real ſaving to our own diſburſements; ſince it was a ſuperfluous increaſe of our military ſtrength, if not required for that ſpecific ſervice. Beſides, it was too remote for diſcipline and controul; and many foul evils, unknown to the ſervice before the formation of the corps which were entertained by our government for the Nabob's ſervice and pay in the year 1775, had originated from this deleterious ſource.

THE opportunities which my reſidence at Lucnow, and a nearer and more intimate intercourſe with the King's miniſters afforded me, of eſtimating the ſtrength of the different ſtates whoſe poſſeſſions bordered on the Nabob's northern dominions, or who might approach them in their occaſional incurſions, impreſſed me with the ſtrongeſt conviction of the inutility of the appropriation of any part of our military ſtrength to ſuch a defence, for which a much ſmaller force of the Nabob's own ſepoys, rabble as they were, were more than adequate againſt a worſe rabble

rabble of any that could be oppoſed to them. But the other members of the Board judged otherwiſe, and reſolved on continuing the detachment; and, however I might feel the inſtant mortification of ſeeing my own judgment, formed on actual knowledge and intimate obſervation, ſuperſeded by private ſuggeſtions; for no knowledge could the other members have had, but from individuals; I was but too ſenſible of the diſadvantage under which I ſhould conteſt this point, if I did conteſt it, in my approaching ſeparation from the ſervice, which inveſted my ſucceſſor with a plea, ſpecious at leaſt, for an excluſive option in the proviſion of meaſures which were required by his ſenſe of the publick danger in which I had no longer any concern. And when I found both him and the other Member of the Council inflexible againſt the arguments which I urged in ſupport of my own propoſition, I ſubmitted; making the repeal of my former orders an act of my own authority, that it might not appear the effect of oppoſition, and produce a dangerous influence on the credit of the ſucceeding adminiſtration.

MORE

More need not now be recapitulated of it than its termination, which was a corrected adjuſtment of the Nabob Vizir's debt, now ſettled, with the growing ſubſidy and other current payments due for the year of the computation called Fuſſelee, which ends with the Engliſh month September 1785, at 1,05,00,000 rupees of the Lucnow ſtandard, and made payable according to the following monthly inſtallments :—

To be paid to the end of Bhadoon,			
In ready money — —		9,00,000	
In bills — — —		10,00,000	
			19,00,000
To be paid to the end of Coar — —			5,00,000
Ditto — —	Kateg — —		5,00,000
Ditto — —	Augun — —		5,00,000
Ditto — —	Poos, viz.		
In ready money — —		5,00,000	
Bills on Surat or Calcutta		15,00,000	
			20,00,000
To be paid to the end of May — —			3,25,000
Ditto — —	Phagoon — —		3,25,000
Ditto — —	Cheyt — —		3,25,000
To be paid to the end of Byſaak — —			3,25,000
Ditto — —	Seyt, viz.		
In ready money — —		3,25,000	
Bills on Surat or Calcutta		10,00,000	
			13,25,000

To be paid to the end of Assar — —			3,25,000
Ditto — — Sawan — —			3,25,000
Ditto — — Bhadoon, viz.			
In ready money — —	3,25,000		
Bills on Surat or Calcutta	15,00,000		
			18,25,000
Lucnow Rupees of 23, 24, 25, and 26 Suns			1,05,00,000

I HAD the satisfaction of learning a few days before my departure, that the kist, or demand for Poos, which was the last due, and which was the heaviest kist of the year, had been completely discharged; and I have every well-grounded reason to believe, that the remaining payments will be as punctually made; so that the Nabob's debt, which, when I went to Lucnow, amounted to 72,95,656. 4. 7. current rupees *, and was the accumulated growth of many years, was now reduced to about 23,00,000 rupees †.

THE

* Vide Account drawn out by the Accomptant-General, and laid before the Board, with his letter of the 24th of February 1784.

† By late advices from Bengal, the East India Company are informed that the Nabob Vizir has faithfully complied with every engagement he entered into with Mr. Hastings—that his debt was not only completely cleared off, but he was actually in advance in his

THE other tranſactions of the Board, which paſſed in the period of this review, having ariſen out of accidental emergency, unconnected with any fixed, and followed rule of conduct, I ſhall be brief in my recital of them.

ON the 16th of November, letters were written to the Marquis de *Buſſy*, to the Director and Council for the Dutch ſettlement at Columbo, to the Government General of Batavia, and to the Preſident and Select Committee of Fort St. George; propoſing, and warranting the means for accommodating the long-depending diſpute betwixt the latter and M. de *Buſſy*, reſpecting the mode of transferring the ceſſion of Trincomale, according to the late treaties with France and Holland, to the repreſentatives of the latter; the Marquis de *Buſſy* claiming to deliver it immediately to the Dutch Government at Columbo, according to the intent and ſpirit of the treaties, and Lord *Macartney* and his Commit-

his current monthly payments: the debt here alluded to is that which was ſtruck out of the Company's ſtatement in November 1783, and pronounced abſolutely irrecoverable by the Miniſter of that period.

tee, to be put in poſſeſſion of it on the part of Great-Britain, that it might be delivered on their part, and by their agents, to the Dutch, according to the letter of the treaties. After a variety of elaborate and ſubtle diſcuſſion of this unſubſtantial difference, by which, if all parties were not loſers, none apparently gained; it had been agreed between the two Governments of Fort St. George and Pondicherry, to refer the point in diſpute to their reſpective Courts in Europe; and a French frigate had been diſpatched from Pondicherry for that purpoſe, in which Mr. *Staunton,* private Secretary to Lord *Macartney,* had been permitted to take his paſſage for the explanation of what had paſſed on the ſide of the Government of Madraſs in relation to this conteſt. We decided, (deeming ourſelves, as the ſuperior and controlling power on the part of the Britiſh nation in India, competent to decide) that the Marquis de *Buſſy* ſhould cauſe the ceſſion to be immediately made by his own agents, whom in that caſe we authoriſed to act as ours, to thoſe of the Dutch Government of Columbo; and we required him in return,

turn, to reſtore the town of Cuddaloor to the Government of Fort St. George, which had been withheld by this unprofitable delay; the treaties having expreſsly ſtipulated, that the reſtitution of all places taken in the courſe of the war, which were to be reſtored, ſhould take effect at the ſame period of time. Period!—an unhappy word, the grammatical conſtruction of which occupied a large portion of the correſpondence which paſſed between the Select Committee of Fort St. George and the Marquis de *Buſſy*, and yet remains unreſolved.

If ſuperſtition may be admitted to ſuggeſt the ſources of thoſe untoward ſeries of political events which the common ſenſe of mankind cannot reconcile to any intelligible cauſes, that which I have been relating ſeems to be under the government of a peculiar kind of fatality; for to a plain underſtanding, there appears to be no reaſon which could have hindered the effect of the treaties on their firſt promulgation, but many to promote it; yet, after the profeſſed endeavours of all parties, and the expiration of many months, it was more diſtant than ever; and when a peremptory meaſure was adopted which ſeemed to enſure its eaſy ſucceſs, the death of the Marquis de *Buſſy*, of which we were appriſed a few days preceding my departure, will moſt probably have defeated the end of that alſo. In the mean time, the Dutch loſe the benefit of their confeſſed right of poſſeſſion; the French have the charge of it without any dependant advantage; and keep the poſſeſſion of our Fort and territory of Cuddaloor, probably with as little advantage, though to our certain loſs and injury *.

My report of the negotiations which I performed at the injunction of the Board, for obtaining the return of the Prince *Mirza Jehander Shaw* to his father's court, contains all that is neceſſary for information on that detached ſubject, and it has already been publiſhed. As an object of mere curioſity, I ſhall however add, in an Appendix, a narrative written by the Prince himſelf of his flight, which will

* The Ceſſions were mutually made in conformity to the orders of the Governor General and Council here alluded to, as appears by letters received from Bengal ſince Mr. Haſtings's arrival in England.

perhaps

perhaps afford more entertainment to moſt readers of theſe numerous ſheets, than the contents of all the reſt.

SOME time preceding, the Select Committee of Fort St. George had by different ſhips ſent round many of the King's officers and ſoldiers to Calcutta. Their motive for this act was probably to free themſelves from the expence of their ſubſiſtence, for we had no official information of the purpoſe of it, nor indeed were we at all apprized by what authority many of theſe conſignments were made. This laid the Board under ſome difficulties. The ſenior officer, Colonel *Gordon*, had received orders from the Proviſional Commander in Chief upon the coaſt, concerning the diſpoſition of theſe men, and for recruiting the corps to which they belonged; and he in virtue of this commiſſion aſſumed the exerciſe of an authority which the Board (having no regular knowledge of him) could not admit. The perſonal merits and ingenuous manners of Colonel *Gordon*, exacted from the Board a degree of reſpect, in the obſervance of which, ſomething too much was yielded of a power of which he was either entitled to the complete exercise, or of which he should have been denied the right altogether.

It is needless to enumerate all the little subjects of altercation which arose out of this equivocal state. It is sufficient to say, that the Board finally decided, as the proper and only judges in such a contest, by ordering all the men whose time of service was expired, and were willing and fit to enter into the Company's service, to be entertained, and the remainder to be embarked for England. To the officers, who were more than a hundred in number, and who would have been subjected to great inconvenience, nor the commanders to less, by being crowded as passengers in the Company's chartered ships, were allowed, to those who chose it, fixed sums as passage-money, to provide their own means of conveyance. An ill judged claim, asserted by Colonel *Gordon*, to supersede the authority of the Board in appointing general courts-martial, afforded an occasion for addressing the Court of Directors upon the general subject of the contradictory and ill-defined powers of the

the Board and the King's military Commanders in Chief in India, as they at this time ſtood in relation to each other, and to treat it with a large and free diſcuſſion.

I NOW come to the chief object of this recapitulation; namely, my ſeparation from the ſervice. Although I conſidered this as an event already determined, having myſelf long ſince fixed the neceſſity and obligation of it by declarations which left no option to my diſcretion, and little chance of their being rendered null by the reſervations * which a due reſpect for authority had impelled me to annex to them; yet as the poſſibility at leaſt of theſe reſervations being verified by the event was implied in my having made them, and as I knew that the Parliament of Great-Britain was, at the time of the laſt advices from thence, employed in the conſidera-

* The reſervation here alluded to was contained in Mr. Haſtings's letter to the Court of Directors of the 20th March 1783. In that letter he deſired they would appoint a ſucceſſor to the Government of Bengal, and notified his determination to reſign it the following year, unleſs he was furniſhed with thoſe powers which have lately been conferred upon Lord Cornwallis.

tion

tion of ſuch points as neceſſarily led to thoſe, which in one determination of them might prove the pledged grounds of my continuance in office, I reſolved to wait the arrival of the next diſpatches, which I was given to expect, by thoſe of the Surpriſe, would ſoon follow in the Fox packet, or in the Cygnet ſloop of war. But ſo near was my ſenſe of this ſuſpenſion to certainty, that I was exceedingly anxious to give early notice to the Court of Directors of my determination in this ſtate of it; nor was it leſs neceſſary to repeat the advice of the loſs which the conſtitutional adminiſtration had already received by the death of Mr. *Wheeler*, of which no information had yet been ſent, except an expreſs diſpatched by myſelf in November from Benares, and intended for a conveyance by land from Bombay. The Surpriſe having approved herſelf the fitteſt veſſel that we could procure for a voyage of expedition, the Board agreed to hire her for this occaſion for a freight, eſtimated by the inverted proportion of the time in which ſhe performed her paſſage. She was taken up on the 19th of November, and left her pilot on the 16th of December.

In

In this letter, I expreſſed my intention of waiting the arrival of the next regular diſpatches from England; but on the 20th of the ſame month, I received a packet by the way of Buſſorah, which put an inſtant period to all my heſitation. It brought me letters dated in London as late as the 3d of Auguſt, and information of a bill for the regulation of all the various branches of the Britiſh poſſeſſions in India, on an entirely new and permanent ſyſtem, which had actually paſſed the Houſe of Commons, and had been received with ſo little oppoſition in the Houſe of Lords, as to denounce its paſſage, with no eſſential change, through that channel of the legiſlator alſo. The parts of it which bore a relation to my office, and to thoſe points which I had fixed as ultimately deciſive of my reſolution, were the clauſes which declared the conſtitution of the Government of Bengal to reſide in a Governor-General and a limited number of counſellors, with the ſame equality of powers as that of the exiſting conſtitution; and which, though it confirmed the preſent members in their places, left their removal at the diſcretion of the King's Miniſter.

The first of these clauses was a determinate removal of the supposition, in the eventual verification of which, I had declared that I would still continue to retain the service and my office, and by a consonant and necessary inference imposed on me the indipensable obligation of resigning both; for I had repeatedly, in addresses to the highest authority to which I was permitted to address myself declared that I would do it. As to the latter, it had no other effect upon my mind, in respect to my determination already confirmed, than to divest it of all concern for the consequence; since the grounds assigned for the construction of the new bill, as I gathered them from printed extracts, and from the concurrent information of private letters written to others as well as to myself, were such as indicated my dismission as the necessary conclusion from them; nor could I descend to so humble a sense of my own unimportance, as to suppose that the declarations which I had made and repeated of my intention would pass totally unnoticed, when they related to an effect of such magnitude, as the transfer of the first efficient authority by which the new system was to be conducted, into hands not expressly

presſly ſelected for it. I therefore concluded, that either my deſtined ſucceſſor was already on the way, or ſuch orders as were to preſcribe the intended ſucceſſion, in whatever mode it was to take place in virtue of the new act. It is true that no public or official notice had been received of the act, nor were we informed yet by any authority that it had actually paſſed; but my private conviction of both was complete; nor was this a conſideration determinable by the grounds of preſcribed authority. My reſignation of the ſervice was left by the power which had conferred it to my own free option; and I had therefore no other rule for determining it than my own private ſenſe of public obligation, and conſiſtency of character. I knew that the Company's diſpatches, which even in caſes of the moſt preſſing emergency had of late years been ſubjected to great delays, had received other cauſes of obſtruction from the multiplication of the channels through which they were now to paſs; and it appeared as abſurd to me, as it would have to others the appearance of preſumption, to wait for confirmation of what I already knew ſufficiently for my own

own uſe, and loſe by waiting, as I moſt probably ſhould, the ſeaſon for my departure. But why ſhould I expatiate on a point of ſo little moment to any but myſelf? If I am conſcious of having maintained, to the laſt act of my public life, the integrity of conduct and the conſiſtency of thoſe principles which I had laid down for the regulation of it; neither my conſtituents, whoſe intereſts even in this inſtance were my leading object, nor my friends, who have withheld from me their belief in my profeſſions, nor my enemies, if I yet have ſuch, who have laboured to effect by violence that act which I have performed upon myſelf, have any right to paſs their cenſures upon me. I am accountable to myſelf alone; and in the approbation of my own mind, I feel a ſupport which the world cannot move. Yet may I feel a regret, to ſee that hope which I had too fondly indulged, and which I had ſuſtained during thirteen laboured years with a perſeverance againſt a ſucceſſion of difficulties which might have overcome the conſtancy of an abler mind, of being in ſome period of time, however remote, allowed to poſſeſs and exerciſe the

full

ſull powers of my ſtation, of which I had hitherto held little more than the name and reſponſibility; and to ſee with it the belief which I had as fondly indulged, that I ſhould become the inſtrument of raiſing the Britiſh name, and the ſubſtantial worth of its poſſeſſions in India, to a degree of proſperity proportioned to ſuch a truſt; both vaniſh in an inſtant, like the illuſions of a dream; with the poor and only conſolation left me of the conſcious knowledge of what I could have effected, had my deſtiny ordained that I ſhould attain the ſituation to which I aſpired, and that I have left no allowable means untried, by which I might have attained it.——But enough of this.

I HAVE already ſaid, that I had protracted the time of my departure, as I had originally fixed it, on account of the appeal made to me by the Nabob Vizir. The ſame cauſe might yet detain me. It was therefore the firſt proviſion which I had to ſecure in forming my reſolution; and before I formed it. I accordingly delivered to the Board a minute, in which I mentioned the probability of my early departure,

parture, and required, as one previous ground of my determination, the pofitive declaration of their intentions with refpect to my late arrangements with the Nabob Vizir, to whom I had pledged my word that I fhould, before my refignation of the fervice, exact fuch an explanation from the members of the Board, and that I would not refign it unlefs I received from them an abfolute and unqualified promife on record, and confirmed by letter from my eventual fucceffor to him, that no refident fhould be fent, nor any deviation made from my engagements, whilft he and his minifters performed theirs in the punctual difcharge of the monthly payments of the year. My minute was communicated to the other members of the Board on the 4th of January, and anfwered on the 14th, by a joint and liberal affurance on their part, expreffive both of their refolution to abide by my engagement, and of their fenfe of it as an obligation independant of the actual occafion. Of one part only they made an exception, which was the continuance of the detachment at Futteygur, which fubject had already been difcuffed at large, and concluded. Indeed it made

made no essential part of my engagement with the Nabob Vizir; and the Nabob himself had seasonably furnished me with a recent plea for suspending the execution of this measure, by the alarm which he had taken at the events which had followed the death of *Affrasiab Cawn*, the King's Minister, of which I may have occasion to speak hereafter, and by his apprehension of troubles on that frontier; an apprehension which I thought, and still think, to have had no just warrant, but which, as he entertained it, afforded an idea of better security to him from the continuance of the detachment, and to the public eye, the appearance of its being dictated by a regard to his interests. Yet as the expence of this corps had no provision made for it in the Kistbundee after the end of December; and the Nabob's resources, of which a large portion had been derived from credit and the contributions of his nearest relations *, were barely equal

* It is something remarkable, that these loans were made in Oude, upon the faith of Mr. Hastings's declarations, and from a confidence in his personal character, precisely at the time that the people of England were told he had lost the confidence of the Nabob Vizir, and of every person in his dominions.

to the ſum already pledged; to have demanded this ſubſidy in addition, and made it payable in the current year, would have been equivalent to a diſſolution of his agreement, by annexing to it a demand which it was not poſſible for him to anſwer. I therefore on the ſame day ſtated the further neceſſity of receiving the clear determination of the Board on this ſubject, and received it in the moſt ſatisfactory and unequivocal terms.

KNOWING how rapid the report of a change ſo intereſting to many would prove in its progreſs and extenſion as ſoon as I had notified it, though my firſt notification of it was private and confidential, and withheld from the conſultations, I had early prepared the Nabob and his miniſters for it, and repeated the aſſurance which I had before made them of providing for the ſecurity and duration of my engagements with them.

As ſoon as the Board had paſſed their laſt reſolutions above-mentioned, letters were immediately written and diſpatched to them by Mr. *Macpherſon* and myſelf, toappriſe them of the ſubſtance of them. Theſe minutes

nutes and letters, with others which comprife the connected progrefs of this tranfaction, have already been publifhed.

I HAD now another point to attend to, which was to guard againft the effects to which the impending change in the administration might be liable, without fome precautions taken to prevent it. The length of time in which I had held the firft office of the government, although with no efficient powers derived from its conftitution, had invefted me with many peculiar or perfonal advantages. My character was known; or (which was equivalent in its confequences) the general opinion of it was fixed: the invariable train of fuccefs with which all the meafures, which were known to be of my own formation, were attended; the apparent magnitude and temerity attributed to fome of thefe, which proved moft fortunate in their termination; and the wonderful fupport and gradual elevation which my perfonal character had derived during a long and progreffive feries of contingencies, fuch as have rarely fallen to the lot of an unconnected and unpatronized individual, from the coincidence of events appertaining to remote and foreign caufes, or to the courfe of nature, with the crifis of my own fortune; and above all, from the virtuous and indignant fpirit of my immediate employers, and the voice of my country, fortuitoufly combining my fate with other objects of infinitely higher confideration*; had altogether contributed to excite a degree of fuperftitious belief, in the minds of almoft all men who were fituated within the fphere of my authority or influence, that the fame fuccefs would crown all my future endeavours; nor let it be a matter of wonder that fuch a prepoffeffion fhould gain credit with men to whofe religious principles it is familiar: I myfelf avow the fame belief fo long as my actions fhall be directed by the fole impulfe of duty unbiaffed and unmixed with regards of perfonal intereft, and even of perfonal reputation.

MY correfpondence with the chiefs and rulers of Hindoftan and Deckan had been

* This will not appear an extraordinary reflection, to thofe who recollect, that the mifmanagement of Mr. Haftings, and the defolation of the Company's provinces under his government, were originally ftated as the grounds of Mr. Fox's India Bill.

 improved

improved to a ſtyle and ſtate of more intimate connection than is uſual in ſuch diſtant communications, by frequent opportunities of reciprocal kindneſs and cooperation of intereſts. All the defects of our government, and the conſequent diviſions and inſtability of our counſels, were known to all the ſtates around us. From all the preceding cauſes it was to be apprehended, that my departure from office, and the ſucceſſion of another whoſe character was yet unfixed, and whoſe political opinions had hitherto appeared very different from mine, would be attended with many conſequences of diſtruſt and uncertain expectation.

To prevent this, I wrote early letters to all our political friends, appriſing them of the probability of the impending change even before it was finally determined, and preparing them to receive Mr. *Macpherſon* as a connection bequeathed to them with the ſame ties of ſentiment and attachment, and united with me in the ſame plan of ſupporting the faith of alliances abroad, while I availed myſelf of what influence I might be allowed to poſſeſs at home, to render them more ſtable and permanent, by endeavouring to obtain for them the ſanction of higher authorities for their ſecurity and laſting duration.

THESE ſentiments and deſigns were declared more formally and explicitly in my laſt letters*, and confirmed by declarations conſonant

* Nizam Ally Cawn accompanied his reply to Mr. Haſtings's letter with a letter to his majeſty, and a ſmall box, or bulſe, which in his letter to Mr. Haſtings the Nizam informed him contained a diamond, to be delivered by Mr. Haſtings to the king. To Mr. Haſtings, to Major Scott, and to Lord Sydney, there could appear neither myſtery nor doubt in this tranſaction, becauſe Major Scott delivered to his lordſhip the Nizam's letter to his majeſty, and the bulſe, with the Perſian ſeals of his highneſs upon them, quite perfect; and with theſe he alſo delivered to Lord Sydney a tranſlation of the Nizam's letter to Mr. Haſtings, and alſo of his letter to the king, in the hand-writing of Mr. Johnſon, the Britiſh miniſter at the Nizam's court, to whom his highneſs had communicated the contents of both letters previous to their being diſpatched from his palace at Hydrabad, and both mentioned having ſent a diamond to the king.—That the malice of a defeated party, or their deſire of vengeance, ſhould induce them to excite ſuſpicions againſt Mr. Haſtings in the minds of the people of England, is not at all extraordinary—beſides, it will be recollected, that the ſame party have accuſed him of forfeiting the confidence of the native princes of India; and Mr. Burke, in his memorable ſpeech

consonant to them from Mr. *Macpherson*, whose conduct towards the Nabob of Owde, which was no less seasonable in its operation

speech of the 1st of December 1783, *published by himself*, has had the folly to say, that Mr. Hastings was "loaded "with the execrations of the natives."—Such a mark of confidence and regard as the Nizam placed in Mr. Hastings, on hearing of his departure from Bengal, as to make him the channel of conveyance for the high opinion he entertained of his majesty and the British nation, was certainly a very strong contradiction to Mr. Burke's favourite doctrine, when added to all the circumstances that attended Mr. Hastings's departure from Bengal, where the regret felt by the natives of all ranks, and his own countrymen, was too palpable for concealment, and could not be explained away. A new and a most extraordinary battery was therefore opened.—Insinuations of the most abandoned nature were made, which while confined to the news-papers were too contemptible for notice; but when the libels daily published were alluded to in a place where nought but truth should be uttered; when it was asserted, that an extraordinary fine diamond had been presented to the king by Mr. Hastings, at an extraordinary time—the affair became indeed serious: for if the insinuation meant any thing, it meant this, that Mr. Hastings had pretended to receive from the hands of Mr. Blaer, of Portland Place, a diamond, which he desired Major Scott to deliver publickly to Lord Sydney, one of his majesty's secretaries of state, to be by him the following day delivered to the king, as coming from Nizam Ally Cawn, the Soubah of the Deccan, when in fact it was a present from himself, to answer some corrupt motive, not hitherto explained. The

operation than liberal in its principle, would ſerve as a yet ſtronger aſſurance of the continuation of the ſame ſpirit influencing our government to all who had the opportunities of viewing our tranſactions with that ſtate, and who were acquainted with the differences which had formerly ſubſiſted between us reſpecting it. Nor was it in letters only that I ſtrove to inculcate and proclaim this expectation, I enforced it by verbal aſſurances to the

ſame body of men, who would inſinuate that Mr. Haſtings is capable of a conduct ſo mean and deſpicable, have at other times attacked him for his boldneſs, and the perfect indifference which he has ſhewn for the event of the preſent perſecution.—They have ſaid that he has come forward to his accuſers in a tone and ſtyle of defiance; that he has told thoſe who are ſitting in judgment upon him, that they have (many of them at leaſt) brought diſgrace and ruin upon this country, whereas an invariable train of ſucceſs has attended his meaſures, and that he has preſerved an empire to Great Britain; and, to uſe Mr. Burke's elegant phraſe, he had vomited forth the proffered pardon in their faces, had talked to them rather in the ſtyle of their maſter, than as a culprit before them, and boldly and loudly demanded reparation for his injured honour—that he had not pleaded parliamentary re-appointments againſt their proceedings, but on the contrary appeared indignant, and proudly angry at what had paſſed; had diſclaimed even the doctrine of a ſet-off, and deſired that every act of his government ſhould be determined by its merits and ſucceſs.

foreign

foreign agents and miniſters reſident in Calcutta, ſome of whom had for many years been my conſtant attendants, and by ſuitable inſtructions to our own.

In a word, I conſidered it as a duty indiſpenſable with the act which I was about to perform, to guard it by all poſſible means againſt all poſſible ill conſequences; not by the oſtenſible forms and cold language of official notification, but by the uſe of every honeſt practice that could be ſuggeſted by a zeal determined on accompliſhing its purpoſe. What remains for the part of my ſucceſſor is eaſy, and I have no doubt of the effect being ſuch as to expoſe me to abundant ridicule, if ever theſe ſheets ſhall become publick, for attributing to myſelf ſo much importance as to apprehend any conſequence whatever from my being in or out of an office, in which I poſſeſſed ſo little of real influence. If the reverſe ſhould happen, I may be as much cenſured for not having foreſeen it as unavoidable.

I shall now endeavour to deſcribe in as minute a manner as poſſible, the ſtate of affairs

affairs as they ſtood at the time of my departure in every department of the Government, and cloſe it with ſuch neceſſary obſervations as ſhall occur to me reſpecting it.

THE political ſtate of Bengal claims the firſt place in this deſcription, not ſo much from its conceived as from its real and intrinſick conſequence. I make this diſtinction, becauſe I know that every ſentiment of my own on this ſubject will be repugnant to the opinions of many, and liable to the cavils of every man who looks only for an occaſion of cavil.

THIS head may be divided into two parts; the firſt, its relation to foreign European ſtates; the ſecond, its relation to thoſe of India.

Firſt, The ſtates of Europe, which I rank in the following order, as beſt agreeing with their reſpective conſequence in India: the French, the Dutch, the Danes, and Portugueſe. When I left Bengal, the French had not yet reclaimed the poſſeſſion of their factories; and the old inhabitants of Chandenagore ſtill drew their

ſubſiſtence

ſubſiſtence from the bounty of the Company. I apprehend no difficulty from their return, as they are intitled to no greater privileges by the treaty of peace, than thoſe which they poſſeſſed before the war. But if the agents, who are commiſſioned to receive their poſſeſſions, are of captious characters, or are inſtructed to make unreaſonable demands, they may give trouble; which, however, may be eaſily avoided by a refuſal on our part to argue with them, referring every point of diſpute to the letter of the treaty, for which a proviſion is made in it; and leaving them to appeal to Europe for any other pretenſions.

THE Dutch were replaced in their ſettlements, the form of diſplaying their colours being ſingly denied them, until they were intitled to complete poſſeſſion by the execution of thoſe ſtipulations of the treaties with France and Holland, which preſcribe that the reſtitution of all conqueſts, made by each nation on either of the others, ſhould take place at the ſame period of time; the French ſtill retaining Cuddaloor. The Dutch received this conceſſion without

without thanks, and complained in coarse and indignant terms of the national distinction being withheld from them.

THE Danish settlement of Fredericknagore was become a great resort of trade, and the chief, Mr. *Bie*, whose behaviour, as well as that of his predecessors, had been invariably humble and unassuming, had lately adopted a tone of independance, and laid claim to immunities in virtue of a pretended firmaun, of which he refused to produce a copy.

THE exclusion of the French and Dutch during the past years of war, and the security with which their ships navigated the India seas, while ours were subjected to great risques and high rates of insurance, had thrown almost the whole trade of Bengal into their hands. To this effect two other causes contributed; one, the exemption claimed by the Danes, and in part obtained, though disputed, from the rigor of our offices of custom; and the other, the assistance afforded them (as I have always understood and believe) by British subjects, under the Company's

protection,

protection, in providing their investments. The former of these causes is likely to operate with a more extensive mischief when the French and Dutch are completely restored to their factories, and resume the privileges of their trade. Nor can I devise any better expedient for obviating it, although I have given it much and frequent consideration, than a total abolition of all duties whatever; for in what way soever they may be modified, the foreign settlements will dispute our right to search their ships, or levy the duties on their trade by detail; and they will of course pay much less than the merchants of our own dependance.

It is true that the British government, having the power, might with ease repress every opposition to its rights, and to the rules which it has prescribed to the navigation of the river Ganges, which is its proper dominion: but if a brutal commander shall refuse to admit the visits of our officers, and ill-treat them, I am not sure that it will be always prudent for the members of government to punish the outrage, although it would certainly be their duty

duty to do it; ſince it would, without fail, become a ſubject of paſſionate and exaggerated appeal from the ſuffering party to its conſtituent ſtate; and if it ſhould not ſuit the ſituation of our own at the time to hazard an open rupture with it, an eaſy ſacrifice might be made of the devoted offenders, and that conduct, which in a better ſupported member of the Britiſh dominion, would be applauded and rewarded, would in this inſtance be reprobated, with the aid and influence of that faſhionable prejudice which aſcribes every act of the government of Bengal to improper motives, and brands the authors with criminality.

ONE example may be quoted to contradict this reflection, which, therefore, I ſhall ſtate to juſtify it.

A LITTLE before the beginning of the late war a French ſhip did refuſe to admit an officer from the fort of Budge Budgea, though his orders were no more than to require the name of the ſhip, and the nation it belonged to. The Governor General and Council, after much tempe-

rate

rate consideration of the case, deemed the insult offered to their authority, connected with the peculiar time of its commission, a proper ground for checking it as a first attempt to infringe their privileges. An order was issued to prevent the ship from passing the batteries of Fort William, for it had been suffered by the delay to pass those of Budge Budgea, until it had complied with the law of the port; and the commander persisting, some blood was unhappily split, in consequence of which he submitted. Vehement remonstrances and protests were issued against us by Mr. *Chevalier*, who was never slack upon such occasions: and there is no doubt that his representation of the affair was not less violent to the court of France: but the war in the mean time breaking out, sunk this with other similar grievances in oblivion. It must be acknowledged, that our behaviour in this instance passed with impunity; but on the other hand it received no approbation from home; and I humbly conceive that such an act ought in the first instance to have been either expresly condemned, and the repetition of it prohibited under severe penalties, if wrong; or if right,

right, not barely approved, but liberally commended.

Besides the difference arising from the resistance which I have described, there is another occasioned by the adherence to an ancient right which the Company possesses, to collect a duty on all goods imported into the town of Calcutta, or exported from it. During the long indecision of the question of territorial right, an obvious policy will keep up the exercise of every acknowledged right which the Company possessed before they had acquired more than their ancient commercial territory, and the Custom-House of Calcutta is one of them. Were this question determined, and the commercial and territorial property adjudged to the same primary charge, it would certainly be adviseable to abolish this duty, since it subsists to the great injury of the trade of the Presidency, which is subjected to a double payment and the vexations of two offices, while the dependants of the foreign settlements pay but to one, and that but partially.

A TOTAL

A TOTAL abolition of all the cuſtoms, with a due reſervation of the Company's ancient right, and of courſe the removal of all the chokies, or places eſtabliſhed for levying them, which no regulations or vigilance of Government have been able to reſtrain from being an intolerable oppreſſion on the native traders, would abundantly diffuſe the trade of the provinces, and by the natural effect of multiplied competition increaſe both their wealth and reſources of revenue. This meaſure is liable to one ſtrong objection: Its effects, though demonſtrable, would be ſecret and conſtructive; but the ſacrifice made to obtain them, would be immediate and viſible, in the loſs of eight or ten acks, which are now annually brought to account from the collections of the cuſtoms, and in the enhanced prices of the Company's inveſtment.

THE Board had taken ſome ſteps in the inveſtigation of this ſubject, but without any ſatisfactory reſult; nor is it likely that they will have proceeded in it in the preſent ſtate of their authority.

THE other cauſe to which I have attributed the growth of the Daniſh trade, namely, the colluſion of Britiſh influence, will ſubſiſt with other evils of much greater magnitude, in defiance of all the orders from home, while thoſe conſiſt in ſimple prohibitions and denunciations of ſevere penalties, without co-operative means taken to enforce them, and a generous allowance for the intereſts, feelings, and natural claims of individuals; without which, all laws will be but the inſtruments of tyranny, or prove abortive.

FOR proof of what I have ſaid concerning the actual ſtate of the Daniſh trade in Bengal, and it may be offered as a collateral proof of the protection beſtowed on it by our Government, I ſhall merely obſerve, that the ſhips which have imported at Fredericknagore during the laſt nine months, amount to no leſs than twenty-two veſſels of all dimenſions, but moſtly of three maſts, and many of thoſe from Europe, and their burthen altogether to 10,830 tons.

THE

The Portugueſe import annually three or more veſſels from China, beſides others which come directly from Europe. They claim no privileges, receive the protection of the port, and ſeem to merit encouragement.

I have not mentioned the Americans among the foreign importers; but as their ſhips have already found their way to China, other adventurers may come to Bengal. No orders have been written from England concerning their reception in ſuch caſe; and I do therefore conclude, that they will meet with encouragement on the general principle, that every acceſſion of national commerce muſt prove an acceſſion of national wealth. Objections may be ſuggeſted to the application of this maxim to the caſe ſuppoſed, but none that will not originate from the equivocal ſtate of the Company's property, which is in a thouſand inſtances hurtful to the general intereſt; and in this particular caſe, it may be a ſufficient anſwer to the objection, to ſay, that if the Americans are denied the direct privilege of the trade of Bengal, they may obtain it indirectly, and to our great loſs, through other channels.

Secondly; of the political ſtate of Bengal, with relation to the ſtates of India, and firſt of the

Marattahs. The peace concluded with the Peſhwa through the intervention, and with the guarantee of *Madajee Sindia**, had received every coincident acceſſion of general intereſt and particular policy which could enſure its long duration; for the general ſtate had recovered by the treaty, all the places which had been taken from it by the war; it had no object in view which it could claim from us, or with which our power ſtood in competition; and it had more of evil to dread from the ambition and rapacity of its neighbours, who would not fail to take the advantage of their being again engaged in a war with us, than they could hope of good from any ſucceſs againſt us. A trivial diſpute had ariſen between the Government of Bombay and the Adminiſtration of Poonah, concerning a petty chief of the Marattah dependency, who had drawn on himſelf the reſentment of his ſuperiors by repeated and avowed acts of hoſtility, and the Preſidency

* In the month of May 1782; ratified in the following December.

of

of Bombay, in consequence of a treaty of defensive alliance subsisting between them, had interposed with some angry letters to save him. The matter having been referred to us by that Presidency, in this state of it, we clearly decided, that their engagement with him could in no case operate against that recently made with the state of which he was a vassal, much less in that of acts in which he was confessedly the aggressor; and we peremptorily directed them to withdraw their interference.

THE minority of the Peshwa, and the degree of independency, confirmed by long prescription, which the principal Jagheerdars, or Feudal Members of the Marattah state, have acquired, and maintain by various adventitious advantages, still liable to be overthrown by the superior pretensions of the sovereign authority whenever it shall be in a capacity to assert them, have created an opposition of inferior policy amongst them, which is more likely to concern our interests in the event of a war, were any other cause to produce a war, than to produce one.

THE power of *Nanna Furneess*, the dewan or minister of the Peshwa, is derived solely from his office, and the feeble and variable support of some of the other Chiefs; that of *Moodajee*, the acting representative of the *Booslah* family, from his high rank and right of territory acquired by the sanction of written treaties; and that of *Mahdajee Sindia* from his military strength and personal ability. The rest deserve no notice.

Nanna Furneess shewed an early disposition to connect himself with the French, and still maintains a friendly intercourse with them. To this policy he seems to have been impelled more by his dread of the ascendancy of *Mahdajee Sindia*, as it affected his own influence, than by any consideration of the general state: and *Mahdajee Sindia* appears to have formed as early a view to an alliance with our nation, which soon manifested itself in effects incapable of being attributed to any other cause, and has produced its substantial accomplishment in two treaties, one concluded separately with himself, and the other

other with the Peſhwa, inveſting him, under the character of guarantee, with a power conſtructively ſuperior even to that of his own ſovereign in all caſes which relate to our nation.

THE *Booſlah* family poſſeſſing a conſtitutional claim to the ſovereignty, a more aſcertained right of ſeparate dominion, and but a ſcanty revenue, ſtands in continual awe of the ſuperior ſtate, and of every member of it around them, occaſionally uniting their intereſts with each, but principally with *Nizam Ally Cawn*, whoſe territory lies intermixed with theirs, and who is no leſs an object of their apprehenſions. Their connection with the Government of Bengal, which originated in advances made by *Shabajee Booſlah* in the year 1773, was continued with his ſucceſſor *Moodajee*, and has ſubſiſted undiſturbed to this time. The intereſt which they felt in it was manifeſted by many ſubſtantial and uncommon inſtances of kindneſs, and though the man who planned this policy is no longer living, there is no doubt that this, as well as every other general meaſure of his formation, is ſtill followed by the preſent administration. The person to whom I allude is *Dewagur Pundit*, who was successively dewan, or minister, of *Janoojee*, *Shabajee*, and *Moodajee*, and the ruler of all their councils.

WHAT was his object in soliciting our alliance with so much ardour as he evidently shewed to attain it, cannot with certainty be affirmed, though many obvious motives may be assigned for it; and as obvious are the causes, though too long to enumerate, and unnecessary to the present discussion, which have hitherto restrained him and the administration which succeeded, from endeavouring to draw any direct advantages from it: There is no present cause to apprehend any alteration in this disposition of the family, and it will be always the interest of our Government to cultivate it.

IT may be proper to mention as a circumstance perhaps not universally known, that the dominion of the *Booslah* family, commonly known by the general name of *Berar*, spreads over a great extent of country adjoining, or intermixed with those of the

the Peſhwa, Nizam Ally Cawn, Mahdajee Sindia, and Bengal; and that Nagpore, its capital, is the central point of all Hindoſtan and Deccan.

Having mentioned the different intereſts which ſeem to divide the preſent Members of the Marattah ſtate, I ſhould leave the ſubject imperfect, were I not to add, that the Marattahs poſſeſs alone, of all the people of Indoſtan and Deccan, a principle of national attachment, which is ſtrongly impreſſed on the minds of all individuals of the nation, and would probably unite their chiefs, as in one common cauſe, if any great danger were to threaten the general ſtate.

Tippoo Saheb is the next power in conſequence. The peace concluded with him has every appearance of duration, though ill kept on his part, many of our ſoldiers and ſepoys being ſtill detained in his hands, and many officers miſſing of whom no account had been obtained. And for them his plea may be, that they fell the victims of his barbarity before we obtained a right by treaty to their deliverance. Some other ſymptoms

ſymptoms of hoſtility were ſaid to have appeared near the frontier of the Carnatic, but may have ariſen from the mutual ſuſpicions of the contiguous garriſons, and at any rate could not have been of much importance, ſince as I recollect, two or three companies of ſepoys had been ſent to repel them. It is not likely that Tippoo ſhould ſo ſoon chooſe to involve himſelf in a new war with us, deprived of all his confederates, and theſe become his rivals; nor that whenever he ſhall have formed ſuch a deſign, he will ſuffer it to break out in petty broils with our borderers. Strong indications of approaching hoſtilities had appeared both between *Tippoo Saheb* and the Marattahs, and between him and *Nizam Ally Cawn*; the Marattahs, wiſhing to regain their former territory wreſted from them by *Hyder*, and *Tippoo* making encroachments on the poſſeſſions of *Nizam Ally Cawn*.

Nizam Ally Cawn, the Subadar of Deccan, is more reſpectable from his rank and deſcent than from any other cauſe. His dominions are of ſmall extent and ſcanty revenue; his military ſtrength is repreſented

ſented to be moſt contemptible; nor was he at any period of his life diſtinguiſhed for perſonal courage, or the ſpirit of enterpriſe. On the contrary, it ſeems to have been his conſtant and ruling maxim to foment the incentives of war among his neighbours, to profit by their weakneſs and embarraſſments, but to avoid being a party himſelf in any of their conteſts, and to ſubmit even to humiliating ſacrifices rather than ſubject himſelf to the chances of war. Yet, if we may judge by events, he may be ſuppoſed to poſſeſs, with an abundance of the pride of illuſtrious blood, a ſound and diſcerning judgment. Our nation has no cauſe to hold him in contempt; for it is indebted to his policy both for the firſt deſign and execution of the confederacy formed by himſelf, the Marattahs, and *Hyder*, which in its conſequences had nearly cauſed our deprivation of the Carnatic, and has left it an incumbrance upon us, which no time can retrieve.

Nizam Ally Cawn both avowed himſelf the inſtrument of this fatal meaſure, and juſtified

justified it on the principle of self-defence against the acts and declarations of the presidency of Fort St. George. The early redress afforded him against both, by the Governor-General and Council, either withdrew him from the confederacy, or yielded him a specious pretext for declining the part which he had engaged to take in it; and from that period we may date his connection with the superior government of Bengal, with which he has ever since maintained a friendly intercourse, and allowed the residence of a minister of theirs at his Court: allowed, for his fears, not causelessly excited, opposed the reception of a successor to Mr. *Holland*, our first minister, on any other ground than that of an occasional commission durable at his pleasure.

Mr. *Richard Johnson*, the present resident, has recently communicated to the Board the plan of a new and lasting alliance which had been the result of many conferences with the Nabob and his ministers, and consisted, in abridgement, of the following propositions.

First,

First, The reſtitution of all the Sircars or Northern Diſtricts, obtained from him by the treaty of 1768, for an equivalent in price; explained to be the ſircar of Guntoor in exchange for all the arrears of the Peſhcuſh; and the others for one crore and half of rupees.

Secondly, An alliance offenſive and defenſive.

Thirdly, A ſtipulated number of regiments, of native troops, to be ſtationed with him for a ſubſidy of 25,000 rupees per month for each regiment; the Nabob in like manner to ſupply the Company on demand with 5000 cavalry; I forget at what rate of pay; nor is it material, as the condition is not likely to be ever exacted.

Fourthly, The *Peſhwa* to be included as his ally.

Fifthly, That we ſhould acknowledge him the only lawful Subadar of Deccan.

Sixthly,

Sixthly, That all other Europeans ſhould be excluded from Deccan and Balagaut.

Seventhly, Confirmation of all former treaties in ſuch articles as were not revoked or altered by this.

Eighthly, That the treaty ſhould be ratified by the King of Great-Britain.

To underſtand the quality of the firſt article, which is the moſt eſſential, it is proper to mention the following circumſtances :—

1ſt, That the ſircar of Guntoor, eſtimated to yield a rent of 2,07,500 pagodas, or 7,26,250 rupees, became our right of property by the death of *Biſſalut Jung*, the brother of *Nizam Ally Cawn*, in whoſe poſſeſſion it had been allowed to remain, and our claim to it ſuſpended, during his life. He died on the 25th of September 1782; but the Nabob *Nizam Ally Cawn* retained the poſſeſſion of it, the circum ſtances of our affairs not admitting of our then reclaiming it.

2*dly*, The arrears of the Peſhcuſh for the ſircars in our poſſeſſion, which was five lacks of rupees per annum, ſtood on the 1ſt of March 1784 at 31,32,666: 5: 4; to which that of Guntoor to the ſame time was nearly 1,50,000 rupees, making together 32,82,666 rupees.

And 3*dly*, The rent of Guntoor, eſtimated by the leaſe granted by the preſidency of Fort St. George to the Nabob *Wala Jah* in 1779, at the ſum abovementioned, afforded us a claim of above ten lacks of rupees on the Nabob *Nizam Ally Cawn*.

Of the value of the ſircars I avoid to ſpeak. My private opinion furtively obtained ſtands on the records of the Court of Directors; and has been ſeverely reprobated. But as I do not form my opinions in haſte, and what has ſince paſt has rather added to the weight of the arguments on which that was founded than diminiſhed it, I need ſcarcely add, that if I were the ſovereign diſpoſer of the Company's actual property and intereſts, I would moſt eagerly accept the terms offered for the releaſe of the

the ſircars with ſome qualification of the inferior ſtipulations, where they might appear to claſh with other exiſting engagements.

THIS tranſaction has been referred by the preſent diſpatch to the Court of Directors, and Mr. *Johnſon* directed to keep the negociation upon it ſuſpended till their inſtructions regarding it may be received.

IT ſeems to have been the fixed policy of our nation in India to infeeble every power in connection with it; and I ſhall not be ſurpriſed to ſee the above propoſal combated on that ground, with others more defenſible. As a general maxim, I affirm it to be a moſt dangerous one; for in every application of it, we inflict a wound on the credit of our faith, and expoſe thoſe who have truſted to it to the danger of falling a ſacrifice to their more powerful and independant neighbours. The Sovereign of Hydrabad can never be an object of apprehenſion to the Company from any advantage which he derives from his dominions, were they of twice their preſent extent; but if any inteſtine or other cauſe of of diſorder in the Marattah ſtate, ſhould leave *Tippoo Saheb* at liberty to proſecute and accompliſh his deſigns againſt them, their acceſſion to his preſent ſtrength would prove more fatal to the Britiſh intereſts, than any other external event that in the probable courſe of fortune could befal them.

THE King *Shah Allum* can ſcarcely be with propriety mentioned among the powers of India. Yet his name and family ſubſiſt, with all the latent rights inherent in them; and theſe are reſpected in a degree proportioned to their diſtance from obſervation, though but little, even by thoſe who moſt profeſs to acknowledge their obligation. The wretched apathy and indolence of the Shah himſelf, render him incapable of availing himſelf of any ſupport, however powerful, to retrieve his affairs, or even to aſſume the direction of them in any ſtate. Theſe have been ſucceſſively adminiſtered by *Nudjiff Cawn*, *Mirza Shuffy Cawn*, and *Affraſiab Cawn*. The two laſt periſhed by aſſaſſination; that of the latter happened on the 2d of November laſt. *Mahdajee Sindia* having caſu-

H ally

ally arrived in the neighbourhood of the royal camp, which was at Agra, at the time of this event, aſſumed the charge of the King's adminiſtration in the name of the Peſhwa, for whom he obtained the royal grant of the office of Wakeel Muttaluk, a dignity of ſpecial appointment, and rarely known in the annals of the houſe of Timur.

WHAT conſequences this new aſſumed policy of the Marattahs may produce, I cannot foreſee; but think it more likely to embarraſs *Sindia* himſelf by the burthen of a ruined country and an exhauſted revenue, than to add to his own power, or to yield more than a title of faded ſplendor to his maſter. I regret it only as it muſt compel him to adopt a ſyſtem of caution, which will diſable him from affording that ſupport which he had promiſed to the Prince *Jehandar Shah*; but in no reſpect can it prove hurtful to our intereſts, or weaken his connection with us.

THE *Sics*, who may be conſidered rather as a ſect of ſchiſmatics than as a nation, have for ſome years paſt taken advantage of the

the weakneſs of the King's adminiſtration to invade and poſſeſs all his northern dominions. For what relates to them, to the King, to the Prince *Jehandar Shah*, and to the actual ſtate of the Marattah power in that quarter, I refer to my minutes on thoſe ſubjects already before the public; in which perhaps more will be found to gratify curioſity, than to afford uſeful information to thoſe who do not carry their views far into futurity.

Of the Nabobs *Aſſof o'Dowlah* and *Walah Jah*, I forbear now to ſpeak. Their condition is not to be explained in the limits of a ſummary deſcription, and has been brought to the full view of the Court of Directors, and poſſibly of the public, in volumes which have been written upon both.

I shall add ſome reflections upon the general ſubject of the political intereſts of the Company, or of the Britiſh nation in India, which I deem connected with the ſcope and deſign of this review, as they ariſe out of the paſt occurrences, or are connected with the actual ſtate of our affairs; and if in theſe alſo I ſhall appear to ſpeak too much of myſelf, let it be remembered, that the whole of this compoſition is in effect a portion of the hiſtory of my own life, in thoſe events of it which were blended with the public. Beſides, I am not ſure that the Company poſſeſſed a political character, or can be ſaid to have conducted their intercourſe with other nations on any ſyſtem of eſtabliſhed policy, before the period in which I was appointed to the principal adminiſtration of their affairs.

I KNOW how readily many will both allow the poſition, and reprobate the ſyſtem, and admit me for its author, for the ſake of reprobating me alſo for it. I am not its author. The ſeed of this wonderful production was ſown by the hand of calamity. It was nouriſhed by fortune, and cultivated, and ſhaped (if I may venture to change the figure) by neceſſity. Its firſt exiſtence was commercial: It obtained in its growth the ſudden acceſſion of military ſtrength and territorial dominion, to which its political adjunct was inevitable. It is uſeleſs to enquire whether the Company, or the nation, has derived any ſubſtantial benefit from the change, ſince it is impoſſible to retrace the perilous and wonderful paths by which they have attained their preſent elevation, and to redeſcend to the humble and undreaded character of trading adventurers. Perhaps the term of the national exiſtence in India may have become ſuſceptible of a ſhorter duration by it; but it is that ſtate which it muſt henceforth maintain, and it muſt therefore adopt thoſe principles which are neceſſary to its preſervation in that ſtate. To explain thoſe principles, and to ſhew the neceſſity of their conſtruction to the duration of the Britiſh dominion in India, is foreign from the preſent deſign, as it is perhaps too late to attempt it with any chance of its application to any purpoſe of utility. Yet ſo much as I have ſaid, was neceſſary to obviate the common objection, to which every meaſure and every maxim are liable, which are built on a different ground from that which exiſts only in the idea of thoſe who look upon the Eaſt-India Company ſtill as a body of merchants, and conſider commerce as their only object.

I HAVE been repreſented to the public as a man of ambition, and as too apt to be miſled by projects of conqueſt. Though the only two facts* on which this imputation

* Since Mr. *Haſtings* printed the firſt impreſſion of this work, the Rohilla and the Marattah wars have been ſo much the ſubject of converſation, both in and out of parliament, that I am induced to bring to one point of view, a few circumſtances, which I think will effectually clear Mr. *Haſtings* from the ſuſpicion of having acted improperly either in the Rohilla or the Marattah war.—Lord *North* was pleaſed to obſerve, very lately, that the Rohilla war was not ſufficiently known in England, till the Secret Committee publiſhed their Reports. His Lordſhip, however, as the Miniſter of this country, either did or ought to have known every particular of the riſe, progreſs, and concluſion of the war, ſo early as *June* 1775. It was commenced in *April*, and concluded in *October* 1774. But in order that every fair and impartial man may have an opportunity of determining upon the juſtice of the war, I inſert the following particulars, which I have taken from the Appendix to the Fifth Report of the Secret Committee. Early in the year 1772, before Mr. *Haſtings* became Governor of *Bengal*, negociations were entered into between *Sujah Dowlah* and the Rohillas; and on the 17th of *June* 1772, a treaty was finally concluded between them, and reciprocally interchanged in the preſence of Sir *Robert Barker*, and authenticated by his ſignature. On the 24th of *March* 1773, Sir *Robert Barker* made a propoſition from *Sujah Dowlah*, that if the Rohillas break their treaty, he will pay the Company

tión has originated, have been refuted on the clearest conviction, and this in the principal

Company 50 lacks of rupees, if they assist him in getting possession of their country. On the 6th of *May* 1773, Sir *Robert Barker* writes to Mr. *Hastings* and the Select Committee, "It is well known, neither promises "nor oaths have been able to bind this treacherous sect "of people to their engagements; their own interests, "or their own fears, are the only springs by which they "can be moved." On the 15th of *May* 1773, Sir *Robert Barker* writes, that *Haffez Rhamet* still declines answering the payment of the treaty; that his excuse appears more to delay time, that he may discover how the affairs of his quarter are likely to turn out: and the General adds in the same letter, "I beg leave to "send you the copy of the Rohilla treaty, by which "you will perceive how literally it has been executed "and performed, notwithstanding the evasion of their "chiefs." When Mr. *Hastings*, and the Select Committee, in the latter end of 1773, determined to join their forces to *Sujah Dowlah*, in the prosecution of the Rohilla war, they stated very fully the breach of the treaty of *June* 1772, as the strong argument for the justice of the war. We were parties to that treaty; and Sir *Robert Barker* bears testimony to the Vizier's performance of all his conditions, as well as to the part the English took.

With respect to the Marattah war, it has been so clearly detailed, that not a doubt remains, I imagine, upon the mind of any man on that subject. It originated in *Bombay*. It was disapproved of in *Bengal*. It was concluded, by a minister from the Governor General and Council. The peace was not approved of

principal inſtance is univerſally acknowledged; the imputation ſtill remains; and

at home; and a diſcretionary power was given to the Governor General and Council, to renew the engagements with *Ragoba*, if the conditions of the peace were not ſtrictly fulfilled. The Governor General and Council took every ſtep in their power to carry into effect the ſtipulations in Colonel *Upton*'s treaty. Not a ſingle article was performed, when, on the 26th of *January* 1778, Mr. *Haſtings* entered that minute, which, in a Reſolution of the Houſe of Commons, is allowed to have been grounded on the Orders of the Court of Directors; but though Mr. *Haſtings* laid ſo much ſtreſs upon the important intelligence he received from Mr. *Elliott*, and it is publiſhed in the Sixth Report of the Secret Committee, this circumſtance ſeems to have eſcaped the attention of many. Colonel *Leſlie*'s detachment was formed, and began its march in *June* 1778. The Court of Directors approved the meaſure. They approved, with the knowledge of his Majeſty's Miniſters, the plan formed by Mr. *Haſtings* for defeating the views of the *French* in the Weſt of *India*. They never accuſed him of breaking the treaty of *Poorunda*. From the month of *June* 1779, and not before, the reſponſibility of the Marattah war unqueſtionably reſted with the Governor General and Council. The Marattah Miniſters required, as preliminaries to a treaty, the ſurrender of *Ragoba*, and the ceſſion of *Salſette*. I do not find that the Directors, or his Majeſty's Miniſters, have at any time cenſured Mr. *Haſtings*, or his Council, for not acceding to thoſe Preliminary Articles.

I much

I much fear that it has ſerved, with others equally oppoſite to truth, for the ground of a recent and great national meaſure, moſt unfortunate in its conſtruction, if ſuch were the cauſes of it.

I CAN affirm, that the charge, ſo far as it reſpects myſelf, and I fear that I ſtand too conſpicuous a mark before my fellow-ſervants to be miſſed, or not to have been the aim of its intended direction, is wholly and abſolutely falſe, as it is inconſiſtent with any motive to which it could be aſcribed of pride, avarice, or thirſt of power; for what profit or advantage could I have acquired, or hoped to acquire, for inſtance, in a Marattah war; or what reputation in any war, the operations of which muſt neceſſarily depend on another, and him either taken in his turn from the roſter, or with a choice divided at the moſt between two or three officers ſtanding at the head of the liſt of the army? The firſt acts of the government of Bengal, when I preſided over it, were well known at the time to have been of my formation, or formed on principles which I was allowed to dictate. Theſe conſiſted of a variety

of

of regulations, which included every department of the ſervice, and compoſed a ſyſtem as complete as a mind incompetent like my own, though poſſeſſed of very ſuperior aids, could form, of military political, productive, œconomical, and judicial connection. I found the Treaſury empty, the revenue declining, the expences unchecked, and the whole nation yet languiſhing under the recent effects of a mortal famine. Neither was this a ſeaſon for war, nor, occupied as I was in it, would candor impute to me even a poſſible diſpoſition to war. The land required years of quiet to reſtore its population and culture; and all my acts were acts of peace. I was buſied in raiſing a great and weighty fabric, of which all the parts were yet looſe and deſtitute of the ſuperior weight which was to give them their mutual ſupport; and (if I may ſo expreſs myſelf) their collateral ſtrength. A tempeſt, or an earthquake, could not be more fatal to a builder whoſe walls were uncovered, and his unfiniſhed columns trembling in the breeze, than the ravages or terrors of war would have been to me and to all my hopes.

I LAID

I LAID my plans before the Court of Directors, and called upon them to give me the powers which were requisite for their accomplishment and duration. These were silently denied me, and those which I before possessed, feeble as they were, were taken from me. Had I been allowed the means which I required, I will inform my readers of the use to which I intended to apply them. I should have sought no accession of territory. I should have rejected the offer of any which would have enlarged our line of defence, without a more than proportionate augmentation of defensive strength and revenue. I should have encouraged, but not solicited, new alliances; and should have rendered that of our government an object of solicitation, by the example of those which already existed. To these I should have observed, as my religion, every principle of good faith; and where they were deficient in the conditions of mutual and equal dependance, I should have endeavoured to render them complete; and this rule I did actually apply to practice in the treaty which I formed with the Nabob *Shujah o'Dowlah* in the year 1773.

WITH

WITH respect to the provinces of the Company's dominion under my government, I should have studied to augment both their value and strength by an augmentation of their inhabitants and cultivation. This is not a mere phantasy of speculation. The means were most easy, if the power and trust were allowed to use them. Every region of Indostan, even at that time, groaned under different degrees of oppression, desolation, and insecurity. The famine which had wasted the provinces of Bengal, had raged with equal severity in other parts, and in some with greater, and the remembrance of it yet dwelt on the minds of the inhabitants with every impression of horror and apprehension. I would have afforded an asylum in Bengal, with lands and stock, to all the emigrants of other countries: I would have employed emissaries for their first encouragement; and I would have provided a perpetual and proclaimed incentive to them in the security of the community from foreign molestation, and of the individual members from mutual wrong; to which purpose, the regulations already established were

were ſufficient, with a power only competent to enforce them. And for the ſame purpoſe, and with a profeſſed view to it, I early recommended, even ſo early as the year 1773, the erection of public granaries on the plan ſince happily commenced.

THOSE who have been in the long habits of familiar communication with me, whether by letter or by diſcourſe, will know that the ſentiments which I have been deſcribing are of as old a date as that of my late office in the firſt appointment and ſtate of it. And to every candid reader I appeal for his conviction of their effect, if I had been permitted to follow their direction: for what man is there ſo immovably attached to his native ſoil, as to prefer it, under the ſcourge of oppreſſion, the miſeries of want, and the deſolation of war, embittering or deſtroying every natural affection, and ultimately invading the ſource of life itſelf, to a ſtate of peace, of external tranquillity and internal protection, of aſſured plenty, and all the bleſſings of domeſtic increaſe?

THOSE

THOSE who have ſeen, as I did, in a time of profound peace, the wretched inhabitants of the Carnatic, of every age, ſex, and condition, tumultuouſly thronging round the walls of Fort St. George, and lying for many ſucceſſive days and nights on the burning ſoil, without covering or food, on a caſual rumor falſely excited of an approaching enemy, will feelingly atteſt the truth of the contraſt which I have exhibited in one part of it, and will readily draw the concluſion which I have drawn from it, even without attending to the reſt. That ſuch a ſtate as I have deſcribed would have been attained without imperfection or alloy, I do not pretend to ſuppoſe; but I confidently maintain, that under an equal, vigorous, and fixed adminiſtration, determined on the execution of ſuch a plan to its accompliſhment, it would have been attainable, even with common talents proſecuting it, to a degree as nearly approaching to perfection as human life is capable of receiving. The ſubmiſſive character of the people; the fewneſs of their wants; the facility with which the ſoil and climate, unaided by exertions of labour, can ſupply

 them;

them; the abundant reſources of ſubſiſtence and trafficable wealth which may be drawn from the natural productions, and from the manufactures, both of eſtabliſhed uſage and of new introduction, to which no men upon earth can bend their minds with a readier accommodation; and above all, the defences with which nature has armed the land, in its mountainous and hilly borders, its bay, its innumerable interſections of rivers, and inoffenſive or unpowerful neighbours; are advantages which no united ſtate upon earth poſſeſſes in an equal degree; and which leave little to the duty of the magiſtrate; in effect, nothing but attention, protection, and forbearance.

But though I profeſs the doctrine of peace, I by no means pretend to have followed it with ſo implicit a devotion as to make ſacrifices to it. I have never yielded a ſubſtantial right which I could aſſert, or ſubmitted to a wrong which I could repel, with a moral aſſurance of ſucceſs proportioned to the magnitude of either; and I can allude to inſtances in which I ſhould have

have deemed it criminal not to have hazarded both the public ſafety and my own, in a criſis of uncommon and adequate emergency, or in an occaſion of dangerous example.

I HAVE ever deemed it even more unſafe than diſhonourable to ſue for peace; and more conſiſtent with the love of peace to be the aggreſſor in certain caſes, than to ſee preparations of intended hoſtility, and wait for their maturity, and for their open effect to repel it. The faith of treaties I have ever held inviolate. Of this I have given the moſt ample and public teſtimonies in my conduct to the Nabob *Shujah o'Dowlah*, to the Nabob *Aſſof o'Dowlah*, the Nabob *Walla Jah*, to the Rana of *Gohid*, to the Nabob *Nizam Ally Cawn*, *Raja Futty Sing*, and *Mahdajee Sindia*; and I have had the ſatisfaction of ſeeing the policy, as well as the moral rectitude, of this practice juſtified by the exemplary ſufferings of all who have deviated from it, in acts of perfidy to myſelf, or to the government over which I preſided during the time that I have had charge of it.

IF

If in this diſplay of my own character, I ſhall appear to have tranſgreſſed the bounds of modeſty, I ſhall not decline the charge, nor fear to aggravate it by adding, that I have never yet planned or authoriſed any military operation, or ſeries of operations, which has not been attended with complete ſucceſs, in the attainment of its profeſſed objects; and that I have never, in any period of my life, engaged in a negociation which I did not ſee terminate as I wiſhed and expected: and let this concluſion be offered as an undeniable proof of the propriety and efficacy of the principles on which I have regulated my conduct in both.

It would not be either an unpleaſing or an unprofitable employment to turn from the ſurvey of our neighbours, and from the contemplation of their views, intereſts, powers, and reſources, and to look back on our own; mixing with the reflections obvious to our habits of thinking, thoſe which would occur to the people with whom we have been engaged in paſt hoſtility, or who may expect to be eventually concerned with us, whether as friends or

 foes,

foes, in future operations. Very different would be the obſervations made by a ſpectator in ſuch a point of view, from thoſe which paſs in the mind of a mere individual, through the clouded medium of his own wants and feelings, and with the terrors and diſcontents of his fellow-citizens aggravating his own: and ſuch, perhaps, as the following would be his reflections, as the different objects of his contemplation paſſed in ſucceſſion before him.

No ſtate can carry on extenſive military operations for any length of time, without impoſing ſome burthens upon its ſubjects, or ſubjecting them to conſequent inconveniencies; and thoſe that ſuffer will complain, and condemn meaſures which create partial exigency, without conſidering their object and tendency. To the complaints of individuals, the adherents of party will ſuperadd their accuſations, exaggerate the temporary evil that exiſts, and darken by deſpondency the bright expectations of a future period. Such particularly has been the caſe in Bengal; and murmurs, ſuſpicions, and deſpair, have been tranſmitted from India to England.

In

In proportion as our diſtreſſes have been, or have appeared to be, preſſing, the power, reſources, and advantages of our enemies have been ſuppoſed to accumulate; and an idea is adopted without reflection, that the cauſe which diminiſhes our reſources, operates on one ſide only, without producing a ſimilar effect on the ſtrength of our enemies; as if it were in their power to marſhal armies, and undertake military expeditions, without any augmentation of expence or diſtreſs to individuals. With as limited a judgment men are apt to draw concluſions from the errors and deficiencies of government, and the miſmanagement of military operations, not reflecting that our adverſaries have alſo their difficulties to ſurmount, which ariſe out of the imperfection of human policy and the depravations of ſelf-intereſt; and that the fortune of contending ſtates, as of ſimple individuals, as often turns on the different effects of their mutual blunders and miſconduct, as on the ſuperiority of ſkill and exertion.

But widely different is the eſtimate formed, by thoſe whom neceſſity has led us to oppoſe or attack, of our ſtrength and reſources. They behold with aſtoniſhment the exertions that have been made from the banks of the Ganges; and reaſoning as we have done from their own diſtreſſes, lament the neceſſity that has engaged them in wars with a power capable of making ſuch exertions, and whoſe reſources, inſtead of being diminiſhed, muſt appear to them to augment. Inſtead of being able to extend their incurſions to the capital of our dominions, which at a period little remote from the eſtabliſhment of the Company's authority they did with ſucceſs; they find themſelves attacked in the centre of their own territories, and all their exertions required for the defence of them. They find, notwithſtanding the temporary ſucceſs they have derived from accident or miſmanagement, that we have freſh armies ready to take the field, and that whilſt our ſpirit is unabated, our ſtrength is ſufficient to give efficacy to its reſolutions.

The concluſion I would draw from theſe premiſes is, that the vigorous exertions which we have made for the defence and

and ſecurity of our own poſſeſſions, have impreſſed an idea of our ſtrength and reſources among the powers of India, which will, more than any other motive, contribute to eſtabliſh the preſent peace on a firm foundation; to ſhew that if our reſources have ſuffered a diminution, thoſe of the ſtates with which we have been engaged in war, have felt, in probably a greater degree, the ſame inconvenience; and finally, to evince the propriety of thoſe exertions, notwithſtanding the expence with which they have been made, by the event itſelf, which has evidently proved to all the powers of Hindoſtan and Deccan, that their combined ſtrength and politics, aſſiſted by our great European enemy the French, have not been able to deſtroy the ſolid fabric of the Engliſh power in the Eaſt, nor even to deprive it of any portion of the territories over which its controul extends.

Revenues.—THE three principal ſources of the revenues enjoyed by the Company in Bengal, are, the land-rents, ſalt, and opium.

The ſyſtem eſtabliſhed in February 1781, for the management and collection of the land-rents, has continued to the preſent period, without any material variation; and the complete information which has been laid before the Company upon this ſubject, renders particular explanations ſuperfluous. I ſhall therefore content myſelf with inſerting a few general remarks.

The eſtabliſhment of the preſent Committee of Revenue, or ſome other founded on the ſame principles, appears to me the propereſt mode of agency that can be adopted for the controul of the revenue department.

The ſyſtem of government in Bengal is ſo complicated, and embraces ſo many and diſtinct objects, that it would be difficult for any ſet of men, who may become members of the ſupreme adminiſtration, to enter into the detail attending the revenues; and this difficulty will amount to an impoſſibility, if thoſe who poſſeſs the ſupreme controul ſhould be appointed members

members of it without any previous local knowledge and experience.

It will be obſerved, that the amount of the ſettlement annually varies, and that it has never been compleatly realized without ſome balance. I may venture to affirm, that this has been the caſe for the laſt century, and that our predeceſſors the Mahommedans, though poſſeſſed of advantages which a fluctuating European adminiſtration can ſcarce ever hope to attain, cannot boaſt of ever having collected the entire annual aſſeſſment. It may perhaps, in time, be poſſible to prevent nearly any diminution either in the amount of the ſettlement or collections; but whilſt the government requires ſo large a proportion of the produce of the country, cauſes beyond the reach of human controul will occaſionally operate, to render ſome indulgence in favour of its ſubjects indiſpenſable; and the formality of agreements will but ill juſtify the rigour of exaction.

With reſpect to the amount of the preſent ſettlement, I am ſo far from deeming it too heavy, that I am clearly of opinion it may, by prudent management, formed upon local experience, admit of an increaſe. I ſpeak generally; for the particular diſtribution will in many inſtances be found unequal; a defect in the ſyſtem, which can never be remedied by any permanent rule, but muſt be corrected by temporary application according to the exigency of particular circumſtances.

THE public in England have of late years adopted very high ideas of the rights of the Zemindars in Hindoſtan; and the prevailing prejudice has conſidered every occaſional diſpoſſeſſion of a Zemindar from the management of his lands, as an act of oppreſſion. I mean not here to enter into any diſcuſſion of their rights, or to diſtinguiſh between right, fact, and form, as applied to their ſituation. Our government, on grounds which more minute ſcrutiny may, perhaps, find at variance with facts, has admitted the opinion of their rightful proprietorſhip of the lands. I do not mean to conteſt their right of inheritance to the lands, whilſt

I aſſert

I aſſert the right of government to the produce thereof. The Mahommedan rulers continually exerciſed, with a ſeverity unknown to the Britiſh adminiſtration in Bengal, the power of diſpoſſeſſing the Zemindars on any failure in the payment of their rents, not only pro tempore but in perpetuity. The fact is notorious; but leſt proof of it ſhould be required, I ſhall ſelect one inſtance out of many that might be produced; and only mention that the Zemindary of Rajeſhahy, the ſecond in rank in Bengal, and yielding an annual revenue of about twenty-five lacks of rupees, has riſen to its preſent magnitude during the courſe of the laſt eighty years, by accumulating the property of a great number of diſpoſſeſſed Zemindars, although the anceſtors of the preſent poſſeſſor had not by inheritance a right to the property of a ſingle village within the whole zemindary.

I SHALL only further obſerve on the propoſed* plan of reſtoring the Zemindars to

* The plan of a general reſtoration of Zemindars to the poſſeſſion of their lands, as originally propoſed by Mr. Fox, and as afterwards inſerted in Mr. Pitt's bill,

to the poſſeſſion of their lands, and the management of their revenues; that unleſs care ſhould be taken at the ſame time to eſtabliſh ſome mode of guardianſhip, with a view to remedy the defects of minority, profuſion, and incapacity of the Zemindars; their reſtoration, which carries with it the appearance of juſtice, will often terminate in acts of the greateſt ſeverity; in the total diſpoſſeſſion of the Zemindars, or in conceſſions on the part of government in their demands for the revenues.

It may not be improper to take notice of the aſſiduity exerciſed in eſtabliſhing a belief in Europe, that the collection of the revenues in Bengal is enforced by repeated acts of perſonal ſeverity. No proof has yet been exhibited to the public of this aſſertion; and I might content myſelf with this obſervation, without adding that the fact is incapable of proof, ſince it does not exiſt. During the laſt four years, a proportion, exceeding one half of

bill, underwent very conſiderable alterations before the later bill paſſed into a law, and a diſcretionary power is now left in the Governor-General and Council.

the

the whole revenue of Bengal, has been received at the Khalſa in Calcutta from the different renters, without any intermediate agency; and I am authoriſed in affirming, that during this period, a ſingle inſtance cannot be produced of any renter having been beat there, for the purpoſe of compelling the payment of his ſtipulated rent.

I SHALL cloſe this ſubject with a reflection, that appears to me too important to be omitted. In recommending the inſtitution of the Committee of Revenue, I mean it with a reſerve, that the expreſs objects deſigned by it, ſhould be carried into execution. The candour and ſincerity which I have ever profeſſed in giving my opinion to the Company on matters of importance to their intereſts, or of even perſonal concern to myſelf, call upon me to make a confeſſion, which other motives ſhould induce me to conceal. I acknowledge that ſome parts of this inſtitution, which depended upon the ſupreme adminiſtration in Bengal for their completion, ſtill remain unaccompliſhed; that even its profeſſed and fundamental object of making Calcutta the place of receipt of all the revenues, without paſſing through the ſubordinate treaſuries, has been defeated by cauſes which my ſituation did not allow me to controul. This object comprehended the gradual removal of the different collectors, as faſt as their ſervices could be diſpenſed with, and on this account only was unattainable. If the ſame act of the legiſlature which confirmed me in my ſtation of Preſident over the Company's ſettlements in Bengal, had inveſted me with a controul as extenſive as the new denomination I received by it indicated; if it had compelled the aſſiſtance of my aſſociates in power, inſtead of giving me opponents; if, inſtead of creating new expectations which were to be accompliſhed by my diſmiſſion from office, it had impoſed ſilence on the intereſted clamours of faction, and taught the ſervants of the Company to place their dependance upon me, where it conſtitutionally reſted; if, when it transferred the real controul over the Company's affairs from the Direction to the Miniſters, inſtead of extending, it had limited the claims of patronage, which every man poſſeſſing influence himſelf, or connected with thoſe who poſſeſſed it, it, thought he had a right to exert; and if it had made my continuance in office to depend upon the rectitude of my intentions, and the vigour with which they were exerted, instead of annexing it to a compliance with those claims, I should have had little occasion, at this period, to claim the public indulgence for an avowal of duties undischarged. But the reverse took place in every instance. I mean to apply these reflections, those suggested by one circumstance only, to my situation in general.

If the interests of the nation are truly consulted, a total change in the system must take place: For whilst private interests are allowed to stand in competition with, or in opposition to arrangements founded on the public good; whilst those who censure the concessions made to them, in all instances which have not a reference to themselves or to their connections, still persist in recommending them; and whilst the official existence, public reputation, and private fame, of the members of the government in Bengal are maintained or sacrificed in proportion to the concessions made,

made, or withheld, the intereſts of the Britiſh nation in it muſt verge to a decline.

ENOUGH has been ſaid to ſhew the pernicious conſequences of this ſyſtem, which is publicly proſcribed, and privately ſupported; which no man dares avow, yet many combine to maintain. To diſcuſs it more minutely would be invidious, and perhaps entail upon me reſentments, which, though I do not fear, I would wiſh to avoid. I have made a ſufficient ſacrifice to truth; my ſucceſſors in office may perhaps benefit by this confeſſion. The duties and functions of the ſupreme government in India will never be well diſcharged, unleſs it meets with the conſideration due to it.

BUT to return from this digreſſion to the two remaining ſources of the revenues, the ſalt and the opium. My obſervations on both will be ſhort.

THE plan for the management of the ſalt, was of my formation. The minuteneſs of inveſtigation employed to fix the ſtamp

ſtamp of demerit on my plans in general, will juſtify the ſeeming vanity of aſſerting my claim to approbation for the ſucceſs of one inſtitution at leaſt, which in its outſet was oppoſed, and condemned univerſally. The intricate, deſultory ſeries of management, which was formerly applied to this department, has given place to one uniform ſyſtem of controul; the perplexity of the former accounts of the ſalt no longer exiſts, and the advances for the manufacture of the quantity produced, and the amount gained, are made to appear in clear, conciſe ſtatements; an uncertain collection has been gradually improved into a permanent and increaſing revenue; and as long as Mr. *Vanſittart*, or ſome other perſon of qualifications equal to his, ſhall preſide over the office, and be allowed to conduct it according to the rules of its inſtitution, I may venture to aſſure the Company of an annual revenue of fifty lacks of rupees* from this department, being the clear and nett amount of a new and ſimple appropriation of a natural

* By a clauſe of the regulating or remedial bill brought in by Mr. Fox, in the late Houſe of Commons, this ſource of revenue would have been entirely given up.

ſource

ſource of revenue to the public ſtock, without tax or exaction; ſubſtituted in the place of an old ſyſtem of artificial intricacy, by which, in the proceſs of the laſt three years of its exiſtence, the Company had ſuſtained a loſs, inſtead of deriving a benefit from it.

THE conqueſt of a foreign principality, which had added half a million of pounds ſterling to the national income; a ſplendid extenſion of dominion; and a large ſtore of lucrative offices to miniſterial patronage, though purchaſed with the blood of thouſands, maintained with an enormous expence of fortreſſes and military garriſons, and the hazard of national diſgrace, with the loſs of it; would have crowned the warrior, by whoſe fortunate valour it was won, with deathleſs glory; and votes of parliamentary thanks, bonfires, and illuminations, would have proclaimed his praiſe and the public triumph. A bloodleſs acceſſion of public income, gained by the ſilent operation of official arrangement, perpetuated in its duration, and fixed in its value by its inherence to the eſſence of the ſtate itſelf, unincumbered with military

tary eſtabliſhments and frontier defences, and miniſtering ſubſiſtence to a whole people both in its immediate diſtribution as a neceſſary of life, and by the returns of a foreign commerce, is allowed to ſink unnoticed in the blended accounts of the general treaſury, becauſe it was not produced by any of thoſe efforts of the mind to which human pride has affixed the claim of renown, and in which every man appropriates to himſelf a ſhare of the national glory.

It is well known to thoſe few who have acceſs to the records of the government of Bengal, or rather to the fewer who may have impoſed on themſelves the heavy labour of peruſing them, that the meaſure which produced this fund was not only of my formation, but undertaken againſt the judgment of all my colleagues, and barely ſuffered to paſs with the reſponſibility of it at my own re-iterated inſtance thrown excluſively on myſelf for its ſucceſs. Surely then I may be allowed to make this diſplay of its acknowledged merits, ſince its failure would have entailed on me endleſs diſgrace, with the aggravated reproach of presumption, ignorance, and warned temerity.

It has also been urged as a reproach against me, that in providing the opium by contract, I have consulted the interests of my friends in preference to those of the Company. This charge, like many others, has often been repeated, and as often refuted; I shall therefore only briefly remark, that whilst the manufacture of opium was managed by the Company's servants in the Behar province, the profit upon the sales was too inconsiderable to be deemed an article of revenue; that the Company, in consequence of contracting for the provision of opium, have in fact derived a certain annual income from an article which scarcely yielded any before, by appropriating to themselves those profits which were diverted into other channels; and that I know no law either moral or municipal, that should preclude my friends from taking upon themselves the charge of an engagement, the profits of which were to arise from their skill, industry, and exactness in the performance of it. It must be remembered, that this remark,

remark, as well as the reproach, applies to a ſingle inſtance only.

I HAVE already ſpoken of the population of the country, and ſhall conclude the ſubject of the revenues with ſome obſervations on the ſtate of cultivation: I am authoriſed by my own experience to aſſert, what every man who has reſided long in Bengal, and has had opportunities of viſiting the countries beyond the Company's juriſdiction, is qualified to confirm, that the territorial poſſeſſions of the Engliſh in Bengal and Bahar, are not only better cultivated than the lands of any other ſtate of Hindoſtan, but infinitely ſuperior to what they were at the time the Company received the grant of the Dewanny, or for many years preceding that period. It is alſo a fact, that the produce of the lands in common years, ſo much exceeds the quantity required for the conſumption of the people, or for the purpoſes of exportation, that the difficulty of converting it into ſpecie conſiderably affects the collection of the revenues in many parts of the country, and in ſome degree diſtreſſes the Ryots to furniſh their ſtipulated quotas

 of

of rent; that there is no country in the world, where the inhabitants in general procure a ſubſiſtence with the ſame eaſe and cheapneſs as in Bengal; and that, if by any ſudden exertion of induſtry, the quantity of land in cultivation could be greatly increaſed, the Company would derive no advantage from it, nor the labourers receive any compenſation for their toil.

I HAVE often with pleaſure expatiated on the peculiar talents of the late Mr. *Clevland*, in civilizing the inhabitants of the mountainous diſtricts of the Jungleterry, or wild and hilly lands of Rajemehal, by a ſyſtem of conciliation which will long endear his memory to thoſe who have felt the benefits of it; and I cannot deny myſelf the gratification ariſing from the reflection, that the exertion of thoſe talents was in a great meaſure owing to the public ſupport and private encouragement which he received from me. In the honours beſtowed upon his memory the Board have conſulted the intereſts of the Company, by holding forth for imitation a character ſo worthy of it. The immediate

diate advantages of his labours are ſeen in the ſecurity which the inhabitants of the adjacent lands poſſeſs; no longer apprehenſive of being plundered of the produce of their labour by a lawleſs banditti, they have extended their cultivation over large tracts of land, till lately impaſſable; and the country at the bottom of the Rajemehal hills, which I myſelf have ſeen in a ſtate of nature, has aſſumed an appearance of univerſal fertility. The remote advantages will be more conſiderable, ſhould the continuance of the ſame plan of civilization increaſe the intercourſe which has ſo lately been eſtabliſhed between the inhabitants of the hills, and thoſe of the low lands. At all events, the Company have acquired a large acceſſion of new ſubjects, who are not only peaceable in themſelves, but have been ſucceſsfully employed in maintaining the peace of the country, and who being warmly attached to us, by the ſuperior benefits they have received from their civilization, may, in caſe of public exigency, be uſefully employed in the defence of our territories againſt foreign invaſion.

Of the buſineſs of the commercial department, I ſhall ſpeak but little. It is a ſubject of too great extent, and involves too many nice and important queſtions to be fully compriſed in the narrow limits which I have preſcribed to myſelf in this ſummary review; yet I cannot paſs it over without a few reflections.

The inſtructions which the Court of Directors framed in conſequence of the act of the 13th, and tranſmitted to Bengal, marked the firſt limits of the reſpective powers of the general and commercial departments; and in fact conſtituted the latter independant on the former. The proviſion of the inveſtment was left to the ſole management of the latter; the ſalaries of its members were fixed; and it was expreſsly declared, that they ſhould not be liable to be ſuſpended, or diſmiſſed by the authority of the general government. The only power which was given to the Governor-General and Council relative to the Board of Trade, was that of ſupplying the neceſſary funds: but this power afforded them no means of controul over the

the conduct of that Board in the provision of the inveſtment, or the application of the money; ſince in the exerciſe of it they muſt be regulated by other conſiderations than the conduct of the Board of Taade; for whatever that might be, the ſupplies muſt be the ſame, and could not be either withheld or diminiſhed without a material injury to the Company's affairs. Yet this was the only power that the Governor-General and Council poſſeſſed. Men whoſe ſalaries were fixed, and who neither held their appointments, nor could be removed from them, by the authority of the Governor-General and Council, naturally felt themſelves independant; and the conſequence has been, that the Governor-General and Council, inſtead of attempting to controul the management of the Board of Trade, have been even unable to impoſe on their correſpondence thoſe reſtraints of decency and reſpect which are due from one public body to another. In one inſtance only has it been in the power of the Superior Government to interfere with the management of the Board of Trade, and in that their interference was attended with an immediate and acknowledged advantage to the Company.

I ALLUDE to the provifion of the inveftment in the years 1781, 1782, and 1783, by means of the fubfcription loan, when the members of the Board of Trade refident in Calcutta, to whom the charge of it was entrufted, acted rather as the factors of the Superior Board than as agents for the Company in their official and collective character.

BUT the power of interference, which the Board exercifed in this inftance, was grounded on very peculiar circumftances which may never again occur; and it is not therefore to be confidered as an exception tending to invalidate the general pofition which I have afferted, that the Board of Trade, in the provifion of the inveftment, are conftituted independant of the Governor-General and Council.

YET in all the late correfpondence from Europe, the Court of Directors feem to confider the refponfibility as primarily vefted veſted in the Governor-General and Council. Whether applauſe or cenſure reſult from the management of the buſineſs of providing the inveſtment, it is to the Governor-General and Council that the ſtrictures of the Court of Directors are expreſsly directed and applied. They are afterwards, indeed, communicated by them to the Board of Trade; but applauſe and cenſure equally loſe their force when they are not openly and pointedly applied, and when they paſs through the medium of others, who may diminiſh their efficacy by participation, but, poſſeſſing no authority themſelves, cannot increaſe it in the conveyance.

FROM theſe premiſes I have demonſtrated, that the management, direction, and execution, of all matters relative to the Company's commerce, are wholly and independantly veſted in the Board of Trade, whilſt the reſponſibility virtually reſts with the Governor-General and Council. This is ſo abſurd a contradiction of principles, that it is ſufficient to have proved its exiſtence without tracing its conſequences. In a former part of this review, I have avowed

avowed my opinion that the attention of the ſuperior government of Bengal ſhould not be perplexed with the intricacies of commercial detail; but it is clearly expedient, that either ſome degree of efficient controul ſhould be veſted in the Governor-General or Council, or the reſponſibility wholly withdrawn from them, and transferred to the Board of Trade. Theſe are queſtions for the Company to determine. I do not offer any opinion on them at preſent.

THE next defect which I have to point out in the conſtitution of the Board of Trade proceeds from the rule eſtabliſhed by the Company, that all their ſervants, according to their ſeniority of rank in the general liſt, ſhall ſucceed to the ſeats becoming vacant at the Board of Trade. This is founded on principles of juſtice towards their ſervants; but it is productive of eſſential injury to their own affairs.

THE general government, and the commercial department in Bengal, which might otherwiſe be conſidered as two ſeparate

ſeparate and diſtinct lines, are ſo blended in this reſpect, that the perſons who fill the inferior ſtations of either, are all choſen from the general liſt of ſervants under the authority of the Governor-General and Council. The buſineſs however of each requires very different talents, and to excel in either, habitual practice and long application are neceſſary: ſo that although removals are not poſitively prohibited, few ever change the line in which they have once engaged, until they arrive at a certain rank in the ſervice; when *all*, whatever their talents may be, and whether they deſire it or not, muſt riſe into the Board of Trade; by which means often the ſervices of thoſe who have made the revenues or other branches of the general department the objects of their ſtudy and attention, are loſt to the Company; and they are thrown into a line where all their former knowledge becomes totally uſeleſs, and they are deſtitute of that which they ought to poſſeſs; probably too late in life to ſtudy a new profeſſion; their minds are therefore diſguſted at the change; and their thoughts are bent on returning to their native country.

If the ſervants of the commercial department were compleatly ſeparated from thoſe of the general government, it might perhaps be proper, when no particular objection exiſted, that the former ſhould riſe according to their ſeniority of rank to fill the vacant ſeats of the Board of Trade. But whilſt the ſervants of both departments continue to rank in one general liſt, ſeniority ſhould be ſet aſide, or only allowed the preference where equal talents and knowledge come into competition. I do not pretend to ſay whether the right of choice ſhould reſt in the Court of Directors at home, or in the ſuperior government in India.

Another defect in the preſent conſtitution of the Board of Trade conſiſts in the number of its members. Four members have been thought ſufficient by the legiſlature of Great-Britain, for the general government of India; and the Company have thought fit to continue the original number of members in the Board of Trade, which is no leſs than eleven. For what purpoſe is there ſo great a difference? It will never be alledged, that the objects of of deliberation of the latter are more important or numerous than thoſe of the former. It will perhaps then be ſaid, that they have a greater detail of executive tranſactions. This is not true; and if it were admitted, I would require no other grounds for reducing the number; for I affirm, and every man who has been converſant in the practice of Boards muſt be ſenſible, that the detail of minute executive tranſactions is more correctly and expeditiouſly conducted by a few, or even by a ſingle man, than by many. The Company's inveſtment was never, I believe, at any time better managed than in the year 1773, when it was left to the ſole ſuperintendancy of Mr. *Alderſey*.

POSSIBLY it will be obſerved, that although the Board of Trade conſiſts of eleven, yet there is never that number aſſembled at the Preſidency, it being an eſtabliſhed rule, that four of the commercial chiefſhips ſhall be filled by the members in rotation. This alſo I affirm to be one of the defects of their conſtitution. The charge of the ſubordinate ſtations ſhould never be given to perſons poſſeſſed of a right

right to vote at the Board; for under ſuch circumſtances, their merits will ſeldom be impartially ſcanned; either their faults will be overlooked, or if party diſputes ſhould unhappily prevail, their exertions will be diſturbed and checked by unneceſſary cavils.

In theſe obſervations which I have made on the defects of the preſent ſyſtem, I do not allude to any particular inſtances. I ſpeak only of general principles, which muſt always invariably produce the ſame conſequences. I ſhall now offer a few remarks on the general ſubject of the Company's commerce in Bengal.

Although we have ſo long been in poſſeſſion of the ſovereignty of Bengal, and have provided our inveſtments, not as the returns of commerce, but as the means of remitting the ſurplus of the revenues of the country; yet we have not been able ſo far to change our ideas with our ſituation, as to quit the contracted views of monopoliſts for objects tending to promote the proſperity of thoſe territo-

ries,

ries, from which we derive ſo valuable a tribute.

HENCE it is, that in all the correſpondence of the Board of Trade, we find conſtant complaints of private merchants making advances to the Company's weavers; of their giving greater prices than have hitherto been given by the Company; of their debaſing the quality of the manufactures, by taking off goods which the Company refuſe; and in ſhort, of their injuring the proviſion of the Company's inveſtment by their competition and interference. Let all this be. It is of leſs conſequence, conſidered as a national concern, that the inveſtment ſhould be procured cheap, than that the commerce of the country ſhould flouriſh; and I inſiſt upon it, as a fixed and uncontrovertible principle, that commerce can only flouriſh when it is equal and free. Nor in truth do I think that the Company, conſidered merely in their mercantile capacity, would much ſuffer from the operation of ſuch a principle. When commerce is left to itſelf, it will correct its own evils. The private merchant, ever quick-ſighted to his intereſt,

interest, will only maintain a competition whilst a profit is to be derived from the trade; and so long as he derives a profit, the Company ought to derive one also. But if in the course of this competition, the prices paid to the manufacturers should rise beyond their just proportion compared with the sales, or if the market in Europe should become over-stocked, the private merchant will soon desist, prices will fall in India to their former rate or even lower, and the stock in the market, from not being supplied as usual, will again be reduced to a quantity more proportionate to the demand. This must inevitably be the consequence, whilst the consumption continues, and cannot be supplied (which I believe is the case with most of the articles of the Company's trade) from the productions of any other quarter of the world.

If, however, the Company's investment should now be productive of less profit on the invoice than formerly, the cause is less to be traced in the increase of the prime cost of the goods paid to the manufacturers in India, than in the great growth of the trade of foreign nations, which has raised a competition

competition against the Company in the sale of Indian commodities in all the markets of Europe.

THIS suggests an idea of monopoly to which I am not averse; because, if it be pursued, it will affect only our European rivals, without prejudicing the commerce of our territories. But it must be pursued not by restrictions, but by counteraction. To find what means are in our power for this purpose, let us return to those circumstances which I have in another place enumerated as the causes of the growth of the trade of the Danes, and I might have added the Portuguese. These I have said are, first, the advantage they possessed during the late war of navigating their ships in safety, whilst our own and those of the French and Dutch were exposed to great risk. Secondly, the facility with which they procured credit in India, even from the subjects of Great-Britain.

THE former of these causes ceased with the war: the latter still exists; and it is there that we must apply our means of counteraction. The Danish and Portuguese vessels that have lately come to India, are mostly fitted out by private adventurers: no great capital is necessary, and little credit is required in Europe for their outfit, as their cargoes outward-bound consist only of provisions and bulky articles, which are procured at a small cost. When they arrive in Bengal, the avidity with which individuals embrace every opportunity of remitting their fortunes to Europe, enables them easily to procure money or credit for the purchase of a valuable investment. They grant bills or bonds payable in Europe at a distant period. They then carry home their cargoes, and convert them into money, in time to discharge their bills or bonds when they become due. All this operation, therefore, is chiefly carried on by means of the money or credit which they meet with in Bengal. But the profit on the voyage is their own; and their nation gains in the increase of its navigation and wealth.

LET us now suppose that the English Company were to open their treasury, and extend their inveſtment in proportion to the ſums which they could procure in India for bills on Europe. I believe it is certain, that if ſuch a meaſure had the ſanction of the Company at home, and the terms were equal, few Britiſh ſubjects would heſitate to lend them their money in preference to foreigners. The conſequence would be, that the Danes, Portugueſe, and others, would be obliged to bring from Europe the amount neceſſary to purchaſe an Indian inveſtment, which would require a capital that few private adventurers are poſſeſſed of, and would occaſion a long outlay of money, and conſequently a heavy loſs of intereſt. With theſe diſadvantages entirely on their ſide, they would have to enter into competition with the Engliſh Company, who, from having eſtabliſhed factories under the direction of ſervants accuſtomed to deal with the manufacturers, and from being able to make their advances long before the ſeaſon for receiving and ſhipping the goods, (without availing themſelves of the influence which they might derive from their being in poſſeſſion or the government of the country) ought to have a decided advantage over all foreigners, and particularly over private adventurers, whose stay is limited to a few months, in providing their investments both of the best quality and at the cheapest rates.

If, nevertheless, foreign nations should still find it for their advantage to pursue this commerce, they must then be obliged to carry it on by means of gold and silver brought from Europe; for there is scarcely any thing else which would answer; the consumption of European articles in Bengal being confined chiefly to the European inhabitants, and of a very limited extent; and such an important addition to the circulation of money would be attended with the most beneficial effects in enriching the provinces under the Company's government. Nor need the Company grudge the high prices which a competition under such circumstances might occasion in the first cost of their goods. They would still receive the greatest part of their investment virtually for nothing; not as the return of commerce, but as a tribute. The sources from which

which this tribute flow would increaſe with the proſperity of their territories; the tribute itſelf would be rendered more valuable; and their profits on that part of their inveſtment which they procured for bills on Europe, would at leaſt be equal to thoſe which induce foreign nations to perſiſt in the competition.

It appears plain therefore, from what I have ſaid, that if the Company were to open their caſh for bills on Europe, one of theſe conſequences would enſue: either their provinces would be enriched by the bullion and ſpecie imported by foreigners, or the foreigners muſt deſiſt from the trade, and leave to the Company not only a *national* but an *univerſal* monopoly; from which the nation, not leſs than the Company, would be gainers in proportion as England would become the emporium for ſupplying all the other countries of Europe with the productions and manufactures of India.

I shall now haſten to bring this, perhaps already too tedious, performance to its cloſe, having lengthened it greatly beyond my firſt expectation, and with much apparent deviation from its profeſſed object. As the labour of peruſal will be increaſed by both theſe cauſes, the readers of it, whoever they may be, for I have written it without any knowledge of its deſtination, will have a right to be informed of the purpoſes for which this trouble was exacted from them; and this ſatisfaction I hope they will receive in the following apology.

My original deſign, as I have ſtated it in the commencement, was, *firſt*, to aſſign the motive for my reſignation of the ſervice; *ſecondly*, to detail the means which I took to ſurrender my place in it unincumbered to my ſucceſſor, and unſuſceptible of any ill conſequence to the joint adminiſtration; and *thirdly*, to deliver a ſummary review of the actual ſtate in which I left the government of Bengal in its diſtinct departments at the time of my ſeparation from it.

The three ſubjects, though thus diſcriminated, will be found on examination to bear ſo cloſe a relation to each other, that it it was not well practicable to treat of the first without entering into as large a discussion of the other two, both successively, and necessarily following it. It is in effect the recapitulation of the transactions of three months winding up an administration of thirteen years. In the former, it was not more my study to clear off the weight of incumbent business, than to fix the direction of it by the principles to which I had invariably, from the commencement of my office, endeavoured to conform it. It was not possible to explain the circumstances to which this rule was applied, without assuming a yet wider circumference, including both the application of recent measures to the construction of those which were connected with them in a remote period of time; the vindication of the latter from the imputation of error, inconsistency, or misconduct; and even the declaration of what I would have preferably done, if left to the free exercise of my judgment in cases in which I had no present option but the choice of proffered evils.

INDEED the nature of my ſubject, conſidered as a vindication, required a larger and more elaborate detail than ſimilar recitals of facts and events which paſs nearer the ſphere of common obſervation. At ſuch a diſtance, any charge may be ſucceſsfully hazarded againſt the devoted victim of *a party*, and more eſpecially of *one* poſſeſſing the reverence of names which ſtand too high for imputation, and holding the truſt of compiling materials for the formation of opinions and acts of the firſt national authority. Againſt ſuch antagoniſts the voice of truth itſelf, ſo remote, will ſcarce be heard; and if heard, will make no impreſſion on minds under the influence of prejudice, or determined by worſe motives againſt the acknowledgement of conviction. I ſhould not have been ſurpriſed if to the accuſations of rapacity, corruption, oppreſſion, thirſt of blood, and other enormities with which the clamour of privileged calumny has aſſailed my character, it had borrowed the aid of contempt to ſwell the foul catalogue with gambling, drunkenneſs, and every ſpecies of profligacy that could debaſe the human

human mind. Equal credit would have been given to the aſperſion by thoſe who on no better grounds have given it, or have affected to give it, to other tales of equal falſehood and malignity; and probably ſuch would have been my lot, had I not poſſeſſed, in the incomparable vigilance and ability of my declared agent in England, and other powerful and well-informed minds, ſuch inſtruments of repulſion as might diſcourage the attempt by the certainty of its recoiling with ſhame on the aſſailants.

BUT however diffuſe theſe ſheets may be beyond the limits which candour may be willing to allow me, I yet hope and believe that they will be found to contain both new and uſeful information. I know not whether I may aſcribe theſe qualities to the following reflections, which I have purpoſely reſerved for the cloſe.

FROM the vehemence and perſeverance with which my immediate ſuperiors laboured during the courſe of ten years to weaken my authority, to deſtroy my influence,

influence, and to embarraſs all my meaſures, at a time when their affairs required the moſt powerful exertions to ſuſtain them, which I alone by my office could direct; and from the great importance which they have aſcribed to points, ſome of which had no relation to their intereſts, and others were even repugnant to them; I much fear, that it is not underſtood as it ought to be, how near the Company's exiſtence has on many occaſions vibrated to the edge of perdition, and that it has been at all times ſuſpended by a thread ſo fine, that the touch of chance might break, or the breath of opinion diſſolve it: and inſtantaneous will be its fall whenever it ſhall happen. May GOD in his mercy long avert it!

To ſay why a dominion held by a delegated and fettered power over a region exceeding the dimenſions of the parent ſtate, and removed from it a diſtance equal in its circuit to two-thirds of the earth's circumference, is at all times liable to be wreſted from it, would be a waſte of argument, nor would it be prudent to aggravate the portrait by diſplaying all the artificial

ficial evils by which a fabric, ſo irregular even in its beſt conſtruction, is looſened and debilitated.

It is true, that it has hitherto ſtood unimpaired, becauſe it has met with no domeſtic ſtroke of fortune to agitate and try its texture, one late inſtance perhaps excepted, which was too ſuddenly repelled to produce the effect which might have attended a longer duration of it. And it may yet ſtand for ſome years to come, though ſtill liable to the ſame inſecurity. The remedy is eaſy and ſimple; but I fear it will be vain to propoſe it; becauſe, if it is not (as I believe it is not) contrary to the principles of our national conſtitution, it will at leaſt meet with very formidable obſtacles in the prejudices which ariſe out of it.

I affirm, as a point inconteſtable, that the adminiſtration of the Britiſh Government in Bengal, diſtant as it is from the reach of more than general inſtruction from the ſource of its authority, and liable to daily contingencies, which require both inſtant deciſion, and a conſiſtency of ſyſ- tem,

tem, cannot be ruled by a body of men variable in their ſucceſſion, diſcordant in opinion, each jealous of his colleagues, and all united in common intereſt againſt their oſtenſible leader. Its powers are ſuch, that if directed by a firm and ſteady hand, they may be rendered equal to any given plan of operation; but may prove the very inſtruments of its deſtruction, if they are left in the looſe charge of unconnected individuals, whoſe intereſts, paſſions, or caprices, may employ them in mutual conteſts, and a ſcramble for ſuperiority.

It has been my lot to derive, from long poſſeſſion and caſual influence, advantages which have overcome the worſt effects of my own deficiencies; and it has been one maxim of my conduct (may I be pardoned for the apparent boaſt, but neceſſary alluſion) to do what I knew was requiſite to the public ſafety, though I ſhould doom my life to legal forfeiture, or my name to infamy. I could verify this by inſtances in which by an implicit ſubmiſſion to poſitive duty and expreſs orders, the Company's poſſeſſions might have been devoted

devoted to deſolation, and even its exiſtence annihilated. I hazarded an oppoſite conduct; and whatever may have been its effects, I have at leaſt had the happineſs to ſee one portion of the Britiſh dominion in India riſe from the loweſt ſtate of degradation; another reſcued from imminent ſubjection; and that which gives life to the whole, enjoying the bleſſings of peace and internal ſecurity, while every other part of the general empire was oppreſſed by war, or the calamities of inteſtine diſcord.

I MAY not expatiate on ſuch a diſcuſſion. I mention it only to ſhew, that if the Britiſh power in India yet holds a reprieve from ruin, it derives its preſervation from cauſes which are independant of its conſtitution; and that it might have been loſt if left to that alone for its protection.

THE inference to be drawn from theſe premiſes is, that whatever form of government may yet be eſtabliſhed for theſe provinces, whether its controul be extended to the other preſidencies, or confined to its own demeſnes; it is neceſſary that the Governor, or firſt executive member, ſhould poſſeſs

possess a power absolute and complete within himself, and independant of actual controul *. His character, which requires little more than two qualifications, an inflexible integrity, and a judgment unsusceptible of the bias of foreign suggestion, should be previously ascertained, and its consistency assured by the pledge of his life for the faithful discharge of so great a trust.

I HAVE said that this is an unpopular doctrine, and liable to be rejected as opposite to our domestic constitution; but it derives its source even from the constitution itself, which requires, in every remote member of the general state, a construction of government not merely different from its own, but that from which its own nature is most abhorrent. The negligences, vices, and crimes, of a political agent, are all totally foreign in their qualities from those offences in common life which the law defines, and against which it has made a provision in the degrees of punishment donounced against the commission of them.

* The legislature has now adopted the system recommended by Mr. Hastings for the government of India.

The

The factious or corrupt member of a council, may weaken every useful spring of government; may embarrass, obstruct, and thwart all its measures; may stop the execution of its daily official business; may occasionally employ its powers for the most pernicious purposes, and still keep clear of legal condemnation. He may even avail himself of the letter of prescribed orders in such a manner, either by a strained or ill-timed obedience, as to defeat their intention, or pervert them to effects the most opposite to it.

THE real character of such a man will not escape the observation of those who live within the sphere of his agency; and to them the motives of all his actions will be known on grounds of the strongest internal conviction, though incapable of direct and positive evidence. Yet it is on positive evidence only that his offences can be proved; nor even when proved can they operate to his punishment, unless they fall within the prohibition of some positive law; although

though the lives of multitudes may have been destroyed, and the safety and honour of the state itself endangered, by the perpetration of them. But it is only by a process of law, and by a breach of some written statute, or know law of the land, that the subject of a free state can be condemned. A constitution formed of a governor, with limited powers, and a council, may subsist under an arbitrary monarch directing it, and be better conducted than that of a governor alone; but it cannot be too simple and unrestrained for the rule of a province so remote from a free state like that of Great-Britain.

To obviate misconceptions, I think it proper to mention, that I allude only to such powers as appertain to the nature of government; not to such as might affect the lives, persons, or property of individuals living within its authority, but under the protection of the law of England. In all cases which do not necessarily fall within the cognizance of those who have the immediate charge of the state,

ſtate, the juriſdiction of the governor ought to be no more than that of any other civil magiſtrate, or juſtice of the peace. It is unneceſſary in this place to treat of the mode of ſucceſſion, or the other dependant arrangements of the general ſyſtem.

THOUGH the ſtate of kingdoms is liable to diſſolution from cauſes as mortal as thoſe which intercept the courſe of human life; and though my opinion of the diſtempers which threaten that of the Britiſh empire in Bengal, may obtain credit from all who read it, yet I fear that few will yield to its impreſſion. Like the ſtroke of death, which every man knows will come, but no man acts as if he felt the conviction which he avows and thinks he feels, the very magnitude of the cataſtrophe may in this caſe blunt the ſenſe of thoſe to whom it is viſibly apparent.

I EXPECT this effect, and foreſee that I may expoſe myſelf to much obloquy by recommending ſo new and unpopular a ſyſtem. Yet theſe conſiderations have not deterred me from endeavouring to render *this last service* to my country, and to my ever-respected constituents; being assured, if successful, of *my reward in the conscious applause of my own mind brightening the decline of my existence*; and of this consolation in the dreaded reverse, that no means within the compass of my ability had been left untried to prevent it.

APPENDIX.

APPENDIX.

A Narrative, written by the Prince *Jehândâr Shāh.*

FROM the firſt arrival of his Majeſty at Dehly* to the end of the life of the Nabob † Zoolfeccār u'Dowlah, there was in ſome ſort a cheapneſs of proviſions, a proper cultivation and policy in the royal domains, a puniſhment of rebellious and wicked men, a reſpect to the dignity of the ſovereign, and an obſervation of obedience and duty. On the ‡ 23d of Rubbee u'Sānee, A. H. 1196. The above-mentioned Nabob departed from this vain man-

* In December 1771. † Nedjif Khawn.

‡ April 7, 1782. This is probably an error, the lunar computation being always uncertain. From more accurate authority it appears, that Nudjiff Khawn died on the 6th of April.

ſion, after a complicated illneſs of four months, and the troops became diſtreſſed and anxious for their arrears of pay: For as he left no ſon, who, in the ſucceſſion of his dignities and honours, would conſider their rights as his own, Mudjid u'Dowlah, who had formerly been a miniſter of the empire, having been confined ſince the adminiſtration of the late Nabob, Mahommed Yaccoob Khawn *, Khowaſs, who enjoyed his Majeſty's confidence, procured letters to be written to the chiefs preſent and abſent, aſſuring ſome of continuance in their offices, and others of higher dignities from the royal favour.

THE morning after the Nabob's death I ſaw that the attendants on his Majeſty were conſulting to ſend ſome perſons to the houſe of the deceaſed, in order to calm diſturbances; and at laſt, † the wiſdom enlightening the world, and all the courtiers, reſolved on deputing me to effect that object. This faithful ſervant ‡, agreeably to the commands of his Majeſty, (whoſe empire may

* A ſervant conſtantly attendant on the King's perſon.

† The King. ‡ The Prince.

God

God perpetuate!) having departed with all ſpeed, and given aſſurances to the afflicted, the friends of the departed had leiſure to waſh and dreſs the body, and the diſturbances and clamour began to ceaſe. After neceſſary preparation, I attended the corpſe to the Musjid Jehân-nummah; and the dues of iſlaum *, as prayers and bleſſings, being paid, ſent it to the place of interment under the care of Afraſiâb Khawn, who was the cheriſhed in the boſom of the bounty of the noble deceaſed, whoſe ſiſter alſo regarded him as her adopted ſon; after which I returned to the imperial palace.

As it was the wiſh and choice of the Begum † that Afraſiâb Khawn ſhould ſucceed her brother, he became ambitious of the dignities and poſſeſſions of the deceaſed; and the Begum petitioned his Majeſty in his favour with earneſt entreaty; but this proved diſagreeable in the far-extending ſight of the royal wiſdom, as Mirzah Shuffeh Khawn, who had a great army and conſiderable reſources, looked to the

* Religion.

† Nedjif Khawn's ſiſter.

 ſucceſſion,

ſucceſſion, and would never agree to ſuch a ſuperceſſion in the adminiſtration; ſo that contentions would of neceſſity enſue. Through the inſtigation of female obſtinacy the Begum would not withdraw her requeſt; and regard and compaſſion for the ſituation of a widow in affliction like her, worthy of the royal indulgence, at length operated, and her petition was, though reluctantly, favoured with compliance. The honours of the ſplendid khelāat* of Ameer ul Omrah and acting miniſter were conferred on Afraſiâb Khawn by his Majeſty; who directed this houſehold ſervant (ſenſible of the ill-conſequences of the meaſure, and the royal doubts) to write to Mirzah Shuffeh to haſten to the preſence; ſo that no ſuſpicions might remain with him of partiality in the rejection of his rights on the part of the king.

Afrasiab Khawn alarmed at the knowledge of the royal favour to Mirzah Shuffeh, and eſteeming Mudjid u'Dowlah of great influence with his Majeſty, made a treaty with that Ameer, releaſed him

* Garments of inveſtiture.

from

from confinement, and having brought him to court, procured him the imperial kindneſs and favour. Mirzah Shuffeh Khawn arriving ſoon after with his army at Dehly, and connecting himſelf with the Begum, who was nearly related to him, and who had promiſed him in marriage the daughter of the late Nabob, encamped near the Turkomaan gate, ſo called from the tomb of Shah Turkomaan. He appointed his brother Zein-ul-Aub-u'Deen, and his vakeel Râow Munny Khawn, to negociate for him in the preſence. On this account diſputes aroſe at court, and diſſenſions in the city; ſo that open war was on the point of occurring. At length Afraſiâb Khawn, ſeeing the inclination of his Majeſty tend towards Mirzah Shuffeh, thought it beſt for the preſervation of his own honour to obtain diſmiſſion from court; and leaving Mudjid u'Dowlah and Nudjiff Kooly Kawn on his part in the preſence, to retire to his foujedarry, Ajjheer. Mudjid u'Dowlah and Nudjiff Kooly Khawn having contrived to indiſpoſe his Majeſty towards Mirzah Shuffeh, that chief, highly enraged, and ſeeing them without forces,

 ſurrounded

ſurrounded them in their houſes*, took them priſoners, and confined them both in the palace of the Begum, where he himſelf reſided. After being guilty of this preſumption, he ſtudied to bring his Majeſty into his own power, and his influence and authority became ſupreme.

His Majeſty, in this ſituation of affairs, directed me to negociate with Mirzah Shufſeh; and I, obedient to the royal will, having obviated the alarms of that chief, obtained for him the khelāat of Ameer-ul-Omra, and manager of the imperial affairs. Much time had not elapſed when Mahommed Yaccoob Khawn, who favoured the views of Afraſiâb Khawn, and by his inſinuating repreſentations had procured the approbation of his Majeſty, ſecretly gained to his purpoſe Monſieur Pauly, who commanded Sumroo's battalions, and the Eunuch Luttāfut Ally Khawn †, perſuading

* 11th and 12th September 1782. Mudjid u'Dowlah was arreſted on the 11th, and Nudjif Kooly Khawn the following day.

† The commander of ſix battalions of ſepoys in the ſervice of the Nabob Vizier, attendant on the King.

them

them to enrol themſelves among his Majeſty's ſervants. He inſtructed them to deſert ſuddenly from their maſter, and repair to the gate of the palace royal; which they did accordingly, and drew over with them moſt of the Mirzah's other battalions *. Mirzah Shuffeh Khawn, finding it unſafe to remain in the city, made his eſcape, and his Majeſty heading the troops repaired to the Musjid Jehân-nummah. Upon intelligence of this event I alone of his Majeſty's ſons repaired without delay to the preſence, and repreſented that it was moſt adviſeable for his Majeſty to purſue the Mirzah, ſecure his adherents and the Begum in the royal palace, and take poſſeſſion of his effects and artillery for the royal uſe. The courtiers regarding the expulſion of the Mirzah as ſufficient ſucceſs, were ſatisfied with their march to the Musjid, and ſoon after returned with his Majeſty to the palace.

MIRZAH SHUFFEH with great alarms being arrived at Kôſee, and ſeeing that he was not purſued by an army, halted there,

* October 1782.

and

and resolved on putting to death Mudjid u'Dowlah, whom he had brought a prisoner along with him; but was withheld by his promising, if he would spare his life, to soften the resentment of his Majesty, and procure for him his highest favour, and a restoration to office. Moved by his arguments he set him at liberty, and also prevailed on Mahommed Beg Khawn Hammadanee to join him, by a promise of the office of Vakeel Muttaluck *.

Monsieur Pauly and Luttâfut Khawn, upon intelligence of this junction, prevailed on his Majesty to encamp at Khizzerabad, near which † Mirzah Shuffeh Khawn and Mahommed Beg shortly after arrived, and through Mahommed Yaccoob Khawn began negociations, and proposed a meeting with Pauly and Luttâfut; who, satisfied by assurances, accepted the offers, and begged leave of his Majesty to make peace. At this time I from loyalty observed, that in such quarrels there was no room for peace; that the force with his Majesty was equal

* An office superior in dignity to the Vizier, and seldom granted but in great emergencies.

† November 1782.

to crush more powerful rebels than the present, who were only a rabble, and dared not to face the royal standard, but would mostly join it, or in the space of a few days separate of themselves; that if at all events peace was resolved upon, they should be called to the presence, instead of being visited; but that if at any rate the latter was resolved on, prudence demanded that only one chief should be sent, and the other remain with his Majesty.

As the designs of Providence had weakened the ears of their understandings, and the eyes of their perception with the mist of ill-fortune, an interview appeared to them most adviseable; and mutual suspicion rendered each unwilling that one should go and the other remain in camp, lest he who went should make his own terms without the other. In short both went, and at the instant of meeting fell, together with * Mahommed Yaccoob Khawn, into the snare of imprisonment and ruin. Upon this event, perturbation seized the imperial camp, and dread of the treachery of the

* 20th and 21st November 1782.

rebels

rebels wholly occupied the mind of his Majeſty. The important ſervices performed by me, though without power, on this occaſion for his Majeſty in appeaſing the paſſions of Mirzah Shuffeh and Mahommed Beg Khawn, are fully known and celebrated. Afraſiâb Khawn, who had marched on pretence of reconciling diviſions, ſeeing Pauly and Lutâfut ruined, joined the ſucceſsful party. I brought all the three chiefs to make their ſubmiſſions in the royal preſence, and they, aſſiſted by Mudjid u'Dowlah, took up the throne upon their ſhoulders, as an acknowledgment of their obedience; after which they were permitted to mount their horſes, and attended his Majeſty to the palace, where they were diſtinguiſhed by the gift of ſplendid khellāats. Mirzah Shuffeh Khawn was reſtored to the office of Ameer-ul-Omrah, and Mudjid u'Dowlah to that of Dewan to the Khalſah Shereefah; but the promiſe of the former to Mahommed Beg of the Vakaalut Muttulluck was not performed.

Soon after this Mirzah Shuffeh Khawn, with the Begum, his women, and all the dependants of the late Nabob, marched

for

for Agra, and requeſted me to go with him: but ſeeing the confuſion of affairs, the evil diſpoſition and treachery of the Mirzah, alſo the diſinclination of his Majeſty, I would not comply with his petition. Being without remedy, he obtained leave from his Majeſty for my dear brother Soleymān Shekôh to command him, and began his march.

It was at this period that much anxiety and melancholy intruding on the ſacred mind of his Majeſty, aſylum of the world, and alſo on the breaſt of this loyal ſervant, Mahommed Akbar Khawaſs was diſpatched to the Engliſh government by me, in order to prove the faith and attachment of the Engliſh Chiefs to his Majeſty. It was my deſign to go myſelf, as without that ſtep the accompliſhment of ſuch important buſineſs appeared difficult, if not impoſſible. It had frequently fallen from the revelation-explaining ſpeech of his Majeſty, that no confidential and faithful perſon occurred to him, who was capable of expreſſing the ſentiments of his heart, and the wickedneſs and ill behaviour of the followers of

error,

error, to his loyal Chiefs; or of delivering to them in a proper manner his commands, and ſatisfying their doubts, or of bringing their anſwers. At laſt he expreſſed his wiſhes equal to commands, to this ſervant, in ſuch a manner, that I reſolved on moving to the Eaſtward; but with the firm hope of important ſervices from the Engliſh, in the puniſhment of the rebels already mentioned. Various commotions prevented me; till at length the aſſaſſination* of Mirzah Shuffeh—the ſucceſſion to his office by Afraſiâb—his chuſing for his patron my dear brother Mirzah Soleymān Shekôh, that he might remain maſter of the imperial affairs, and continue the mode of error—came to paſs. Theſe various quarrels of the uſurpers had occaſioned the greateſt confuſion in the public affairs, and numerous diſtreſſes and injuries were felt by his Majeſty; and on account of my known regard to the Engliſh for their virtues and loyalty, various inſtances of their hatred and diſlike were ſhewn to myſelf; and as far as they could, they neglected no

* Mirzah Shuffeh was aſſaſſinated by Mahommed Beg Hammadannee on the 23d of September 1783.

insult to me, bound in the same difficulties with my sovereign.

Driven by necessity, for the restoration of affairs, and in obedience to the commands of the glorious presence, I laid my plan for escaping from the palace, and confided it to Moāzem u'Dowlah, the governor *. This Ameer, who is nearly related to his Majesty, was from his infancy cherished in the bosom of my favour, and the confidant of this devoted to the royal pleasure. I had ever esteemed him my firm friend and trusty counsellor, and depended upon his loyalty to his Majesty; for several times, when secrets were agitated in the presence, in the Assud Bastion, he was fully informed of his Majesty's desires. I requested that he might convey me out of the palace, or into Noorghur, which joins to it, and was under his care; from whence I could prosecute my journey to the English Chiefs. He from his base mind, and regard to the relation which he bore to Koottub-u'-deen Khawn, the son-in-law of Mudjid-u'Dowlah, communicated my secret to that minister; who questioned the

* Of the palace, or citadel.

news-

news-writer of the Nabob Vizier, if I had ſet on foot any negociations with his maſter, which he denied. He then informed his Majeſty, who gueſſed that his own inclination had proved the incitement of this deſign; but to prevent ſuſpicions of himſelf, he went with Mudjid u'Dowlah to view the ſtate of the Fort, under pretence of the numerous robberies of the Goojers, and other thieves. I ſeeing that my ſecret was betrayed, in order to remove further ſuſpicions of my deſigns, pointed out to his Majeſty many unknown breaches in the walls, and uſed great activity in ordering their repair; ſo that for the following eight months ſuch a degree of incaution poſſeſſed every one, that all ſuſpicion of my deſign was done away from their minds, and they even accuſed my betrayer of falſehood.

At length, having certain accounts of the Governor General's arrival at Lucknow*, I was convinced that no better opportunity could ever occur for my going to him, to diſcloſe the wiſhes of his Majeſty, and

* 27th March, 1784.

for

for bringing about the recovery of the royal affairs, becauſe the wiſdom and loyalty of the Governor exceed thoſe of every other ſubject.

I DID not think it adviſeable to entruſt my deſign to any perſon, but the faithful Mukkurrim u'Dowlah, brother to my moſt honoured parent the Begum Tâaje Mâhal, who by the aſſiſtance of Abdul Rhamân Khowaſs, Ummuldar of my Jagheer at Pâkul, the reſidence of ſome Goojer Chiefs, collected a number of horſe and foot of that tribe to attend me, and my departure was fixed for the night of the 23d* of Jemmâd-ul-Awel. The place of my reſidence was compoſed of various courts, at each of which were ſtationed porters and guards of his Majeſty, who watched conſtantly the proceedings of my family, and uſed even to come ſeveral times in the night while I ſlept to enquire about my motions; ſo that with ſuch ſpies upon me it was very difficult to effect my purpoſe. Thus ſituated, I deſired the retired in the concealment of chaſtity and purity,

* 14th April 1784.

Kuttulluk Sultan Begum, who had been for twelve months privy to my design, and had sacredly promised to keep it secret, that no one might enter my chamber, and that she would say, I was indisposed. When four Gurries * of the night were past, the sky grew cloudy, and it became so dark, that the hand could not be perceived. I arose, and in the room of long drawers put on jungehs †, and girded my waist with a turban and silk loongeh ‡, given me by the head of holy teachers, and chief of the pious Môlwee Fukher u'deen, who is the chosen of God, and a blessing to the age. Upon my head I put a linen cap, over which I tied a shawl handkerchief under my chin: over all I wore two black shawls in the manner of a koit. About five Gurries of the night being past, I ascended to the terrace of my house, and from thence passed from terrace to terrace to the Fyez Naher §, which runs over the wall of the garden Hyaut-Buksh. Here

* About eight o'clock.

† Short and tight breeches reaching but half way down the thigh.

‡ A cloth passed round the loins.

§ Aqueduct.

not finding thoſe whom I expected to wait for me * agreeably to appointment, I began to ſearch about, but in vain. At length deſpairing, I returned towards my own terrace, that I might, ſhould they from dread of danger have deſerted me, be informed of it; or if I ſhould find them on the way, bring them back with me. When I had advanced near the terrace, I perceived a man, and thinking he might be a centinel led by the ſound of my feet to follow me, I ran and ſeized him violently by the throat, when he exclaimed I am Abdul Rhamân, your ſervant. Taking him along with me, I returned. Such was the darkneſs of the night, and the violence of the wind, that Abdul Rhamân ſtumbled on the roof of a bath, and fell in. I helped him out with difficulty, and then went to the Fyez Naher. When I had paſſed half way through it, I perceived another figure cloathed in black, and ſeizing him by the throat, aſked who he was. By his voice I knew him to be Sâbit Khawn, and deſired him to follow me. In the Fyez Naher

* Mirza Imaum Bukſh, Abdul Rhamân, Sabit Rhamân, Meer Ayum, Shekh Fyezulla, and Bukſhy Allah Beg.

there was a wall at the place fixed for my going out, which I had three days before broke through, and made a window large enough to admit me, from which I now descended on a spot adjoining to my armory. Here, under the rampart of the Fort facing the Jumna *, I found the four remaining persons appointed to meet me. Imaum Bukfh Khawn before my arrival had made a rope ladder, and fixed it to the battlements of the Fort wall, which is twenty-two dirrehs † in height, and I haftened to defcend. Firft I commanded Bukfhy Allah Beg to defcend, and after him Sâbit Khawn. Next I began to defcend myfelf, and had got half way, when one twift of the rope broke. I then recommended myfelf to God, and making myfelf light by the fcience of Hittubbafs (holding the breath) flipped fafe by the bleffing of God to the end of the rope to the ground. Imaum Bukfh then repairing the rope, came down, and after him Séhkh Abdul Rhamân, and Meer Aazim. Shekh Fyezullah I commanded to ftay behind and efface every trace of my efcape,

* The river Jumna.

† Sixty feet and a half. One dirreh is 33 inches.

then

then to retire to his houſe by the way he had come, and to follow me at leiſure.

It had been ſettled that ſome Goojers, to ſhew me the road, ſhould attend me near Neelah Chuttery, which is under Noorghur, and that Mukkirrum u'Dowlah ſhould wait for me at Putter Gunge Ghaut with five hundred men; alſo that Abdul Rhamân ſhould be ready with my own horſe at about an arrow's flight from the place of my deſcent. Mukkurrim u'Dowlah, as agreed upon, had left his houſe with the Goojers at about four Gurries of the night, and reached the Sand near the Neelah Baſtion, which is at the extremity of the city wall; when rain, lightning, and clouds of duſt, prevented their proceeding, and the Goojers, unable to ſtand the ſtorm, would not advance, though earneſtly entreated by Mukkurrim u'Dowlah, but ininſtead of liſtening to him, began to inſult and threaten him. Unmoved by threats, he ſtood his ground with only two horſemen. From the decrees of Providence, againſt which human reaſon has no remedy, Abdul Rhamân, with ſome things belonging to me, fled with that wretched band. Mukkurrim u'Dowlah, who had now with him only two perſons, conſulted with them how to act; and it being determined to go back, he returned to his own houſe with a regretful and ſad heart. I had about this time entered the ditch of the Fort with my five attendants: at about twenty paces from the place of my deſcent was the guard of the private watch on one ſide, and on the other a guard of his Majeſty's red battalion ſtationed with Ahmed Ally Khawn. At the ſound of our feet a centinel cried out, "Take care, and attend to every "noiſe." They anſwered, "We are "watchful." I was between both guards, and relying on the protection of the Divine Being, picked my way, ſtep by ſtep, under the wall of the Fort, towards the bridge of Noorghur; but though I endeavoured to prevent the noiſe of my feet, it was impoſſible, as the ditch was full of dried leaves; ſo that at laſt I drew my ſword, and ruſhing between the two guards, reſolved, if any one ſhould challenge me, to kill him; but by God's bleſſing, notwithſtanding the ſound of ſo many ſteps, no alarm was given, ſo that probably they were frightened, and thought it beſt to be ſilent. I reached the place

place appointed for Abdul Rhamân to wait for me, and made ſignals and noiſes; but received no anſwer: after which I went to the bridge of Noorghur, and called out, but no reply was given. As the river flowed under the bridge, I waded through it up to my middle, and arrived at Neelah Chutteree, the laſt expected place of meeting any one; but not a perſon could I find. I ſtood here ſome time to wait for the Goojers; but ſeeing no ſign of them, and at laſt deſpairing, with much labour and difficulty I proceeded through Melon Beds, and three inlets of the Jumna, to the Neelah Baſtion, which was near three coſe *; but ſaw no one. My mind became now very uneaſy, and each of my attendants offered advice agreeable to his ability; that I ſhould go to Mudjid u'Dowlah or Afraſiâb Khawn, who would procure from his Majeſty forgiveneſs of my faults, and my life would be ſafe, though thoſe of my ſervants might be ſacrificed; or that I ſhould repair to Ahmed Ally Khawn, who would convey me privately into the Fort; for independently of the danger of enemies,

* Six miles.

and the beasts of the desert, there was in remaining longer cause of dread from robbers and murderers. I answered them all, that nothing remained in my view but death; that I could never submit to the insults of my enemies, to which I preferred death; that if I had strength in my feet, I would walk to Tughlimabad, a settlement of Goojers, seven cose distant, and trust for the rest to the graciousness of God. Giving not fortitude from my hands, I remained in this dangerous spot, and sent Meer Azim to enquire after Mukkurrim u'Dowlah, and if he was at his own house, to bring him to me; after which I uncovered my head, and prostrated myself in prayer to God, with much earnestness and sincerity of heart. After three Gurries, by permission of the Almighty, a man's voice struck my ear; when I lifted myself from the ground, and tried those who were approaching by a particular call, which they answered, and approached; but the night was so dark, and the wind so violent, that till they came close to me, I could not distinguish who they were. One was Mahommed Azim, and the other Ahmud Khawn, from whom I learnt that Mukkurrim

kurrim u'Dowlah was following them with ſeven attendants, and ſuch horſes as he could bring from his houſe. Soon after this he arrived with Goojer Khawn, whom I requeſted to ſhew me a ford of the river from Patter Ghaut. He informed me, that he was ignorant of that road, but could lead me a way by Raaj Ghaut, towards which I proceeded. On the road the watch of the night cried, "Who are paſſing?" And my companion anſwered, "We are Afra-"ſiab's ſoldiers, and go againſt the Sics."—At length, with a thouſand difficulties, we got over four inlets of the Jumna full of mud; and in our ſearch for the ford, which we could not find from the darkneſs of the night, paſſed through ſeveral cultivated fields, in one of which we found a huſbandman watching his crop, and by his guidance croſſed the river. * I once reſolved

* This paſſage ſeems ſo repugnant to the feelings of humanity, and ſo contrary to the real character of the illuſtrious writer, that I ſhould have been tempted to ſuppreſs it, if I could reconcile the ſuppreſſion to my regard for truth, although even this principle may ſuffer by impreſſing the reader with an opinion which I know to be foreign from the temper and diſpoſition of the Prince, which has in its compoſition as much of the

resolved to kill the guide, lest he should inform the enemy of my route; but on reflection

the milk of human kindness as any character that I have ever known. I was myself so much hurt by it, that I took the liberty to ask the Prince, with that tenderness requisite to the censure implied by the question, what were his motives, and especially whether the guide performed this service freely or by force. The Prince answered, that the man was pressed, but did not provoke violence by resistance.—He said cooly, "I believe that I ought to have put the man to death, "as by the forbearance of this caution I left it in the "power of an individual to defeat my purpose, by be-"traying me, and with it to expose my life to the most "desperate extremity, having resolved to sacrifice it "if any attempt was made to stop me, and I could no "other ways escape the ignominy of being carried "back a prisoner; but I did not approve it, and prefer-"red to recommend myself to the care of Providence, "and suffered him to escape. In effect," added he, "the man justified my suspicion, for he instantly went "to the nearest guard, and gave information of my "route, as I learnt soon after; but I made such speed, "that my pursuers could not overtake me." It should be observed, that the Prince considered himself as embarked in a design, on the event of which the fortunes of his house, and even of a great empire, depended, with which the life of an individual was not to be placed in competition, and no doubt this sentiment was strongly urged by his less feeling attendants; for his reply indicated a misconception of the drift of my question, and was not so much intended to justify his first impulse, as to palliate the supposed weakness of having opposed to it the dictates of his own clemency.

I cannot

reflection ſpared him, relying on the protection of God, the divine preſerver, and went on to Liſſoundah, the Jagheer of my mother, five coſe from Dehly; where I put on my proper apparel, as Goojer Khawn requeſted I would halt a little, and he would procure ſome horſemen to attend me. He accordingly ſoon brought Jiſſoo Sing, who was his brother by exchange of turbans, and conducted me to Serrôra, ten coſe from Dehly.

I cannot more ſtrongly illuſtrate this inference than by the following extract of a letter written to me by Mr. Fowke, the reſident at Benaris, who certainly did not write for the purpoſe of furniſhing me with ſuch an evidence, and which exhibits a trait of character totally foreign from that which might be deduced from the paſſage which I have thus explained, had it paſſed without a comment. W. H.

"I attended him (the Prince) to the Eidgah, for "there is one here, on the day of the Eid, with all the "principal people, both Europeans and natives. It "is, you know, a part of the ceremony that he ſhould "kill the goats and the camel with his own hand. "From a reflection he made, after it was over, of the "injuſtice of depriving any animal of life, I imagine "he was ſtruck with this ſcene. Indeed, the convul"ſions of an animal of a camel's ſize, expiring by the "opening of a ſingle artery, and the livid appearance of "the tongue and blubber, which at that time it throws "out of its mouth, preſent the idea of death in as "ſhocking colours as the deſtruction of any thing not "human can well ſuggeſt."

Jiſſoo

Jiſſoo Sing here brought to me Oudah Kirrum, and other Goojir Zeemindars of the place, who were related to him. Here I performed my ablutions, and my morning devotions. Oudah Kirrum repreſented that it would be better for me to repoſe here all day, and that at night he and his people would attend my ſtirrup, and conduct me to a Ghaut of the Ganges, to ſee me ſafely over that river. I obſerved, "How could I halt, "ſince a detachment of my enemies would "certainly come after me in purſuit?" He replied, "We are two hundred horſe-"men. Fifty of us will engage the pur-"ſuers, and the reſt will remain with your "highneſs while you take repoſe." In compliance with their requeſts, I reſted the whole day; and mounting about half an hour before ſun-ſet, travelled all night, and at dawn of morning arrived at Aurungabad, forty coſe from Sorrôra, where I ſaid morning prayers. Oudah Kirrum here ſent to me his ſon, with Nunſing Goojer, who had lately become a Sic *: and they having paid their reſpects, requeſted I would enter the Fort of Sirrabad; to which I re-

* A religious ſect inhabiting the province of Punjaub.

plied,

plied, that it was not agreeable to me, but I would go from regard to their desires. Accordingly I went, and there the son desired that I would go to Perrechut Ghur, and make one or two halts; to which I replied, it was not agreeable, and that I would cross the Ganges that day.—As they continued their importunities, I put my hand upon my sword, and relying on God, declared that any one who should oppose my departure would give away his life to the winds of annihilation. The Divine Being so impressed their minds with dread, that they now came to me with the utmost humility, and declared, with solemn oaths, that they meant nothing but dutiful attention. Upon this I complied with their wishes to remain till mid-day, and proceeded on after prayer. At length, by the divine blessing, I reached the Ganges, which is about twenty cose from the Fort of Sirrabad, and crossed the river at the Ghaut of Kummir-u-deen-Nuggur, said my evening prayers, and returned thanks to God for his mercies. As from fatigue, sustained both day and night, together with the excessive heat of the sun, a feverish symptom shewed itself on my person, and I had been seized

ſeized while croſſing the river with a fainting fit, from which I ſoon recovered, I waited till one Ghurry of the night, and then proceeded to Suddamunnah, about four coſe from the Ghaut. The next morning Jemmaut Sing Goojer, Foudejar of the place, came to pay his reſpects, and preſented me with a mare. Having repoſed here all day, I ſet off about five o'clock, and came to Putchra-noo, in the country of the Vizier, about eight at night. In the morning I marched to the town of Omerooh, about twelve coſe; and the chief inhabitants of the place preſented Nuzzirs agreeable to their conditions. After ſpending the night in repoſe, I moved at dawn to Morâdabâd, about thirteen coſe, and upon the arrival of my ſuite near the houſe of the late Dundee Khawn *, his ſon, the worthy of favour, engaged to the utmoſt of his ability in providing for my entertainment; and I took up my lodging in the houſe of the Dewan Kâeen Mull, a ſtately edifice, where I remained one day. I then proceeded ten coſe to Rampoor †, the

* A Rohilla chief.

† The capital of the diſtrict of that name, the only remaining territory of the Rohillas lying North of the Ganges.

the chief of which place, Fyezullah Khawn, had ſet out to meet me, but from the miſtake of the guides, my ſuite going a wrong road, I came ſuddenly into the houſe of Fyezulla Khawn; and as I had no acquaintance with any one, all were aſtoniſhed at ſeeing a ſingle horſeman enter freely the palace of their chief. By accident there happened to be preſent Moâtimud-u'Dowlah, the ſon of the late nobleman of that title, Yâcoob Ally Khawn, an ancient ſervant of the royal houſehold. He knew me at a diſtance, and running up kiſſed my feet, pointing me out to Fyezulla Khawn, who immediately advanced, kiſſed my ſtirrup, and conducting me into his Dewân*, ſeated me on a rich muſnud, after which he offered me a nuzzir of one and twenty mohurs, and his ſons and followers made their offerings according to their ranks. While I remained at Rampoor, Fyezullah Khawn ſhewing the proper reſpect and ſubmiſſion, regarded my approbation as his chief bleſſing. He preſented me with two thouſand rupees, two elephants, and ſeveral horſes and tents, with proper carriage.

* Hall of audience.

After

After two days I marched to Tukkia, three cose from Rampoor, and from thence to Ameer Gunge. On Friday, the 2d* of Jemmaud-u'Sani, I pitched my tents at Barelly, and took up my residence for two days in the house of Mânroy. Roy Roopnarain, and Roy Sadooram, relations of Rajah Soorut Sing, who governs the country on the part of the Vizier, came and attended me. The next day the Rajah himself came to pay his respects, and presented a female elephant, with the sum of five thousand rupees, and I honoured him with a doputta † worn by myself. Rajah Jagganaut, his relation, was also favoured with a pair of shawls. On this day also arrived Sheikh Fyezulla, whom I had left behind to remove the rope ladder, and destroy every trace of my escape. The 3d ‡ day, being the 5th of the month, I marched from Barelly, and encamped at Fereedpore, the chief inhabitants of which paid their respects. On the 6th I moved ten cose to Kuttereh, and on the 7th proceeded to the house of the late Moâtimud-

* 23d April.

† A cloth of two folds, used as a sash.

‡ 28th April.

u'Dowlah

u'Dowlah, in the town of Shahjehanpore. Here arrived addreſſes from my brothers, dear as life, the chief of nobles of high rank, the pillar of the pillars of ſtate, the ſupport of the empire, the Nabob Vizier ul Momâlic, and the nobleſt of nobles Ameer ul Momâlic; Mr. Haſtings, with the copy of an imperial ſhookeh*. The alarms of both, occaſioned by the contents of the ſhookeh, concerning my march, appeared fully, and I immediately anſwered their addreſſes, by diſcloſing the real wiſhes of his Majeſty, and ſhewing that he had written contrary to them, merely to pleaſe the minds of his refractory ſervants, that both might be relieved from their anxiety. On the 8th I marched thirteen coſe, and encamped near Serromunnagur, and on the 9th † to Dirga Gunge, which was a very long ſtage. From thence I moved to Bugwantnuggur, where I halted two days out of tenderneſs for my followers, who were all much wearied with ſucceſſive marches. What is extraordinary, the road on this day's march is much infeſted with

* A letter from the king under the privy ſeal.

† 30th April.

banditti, who plunder and murder caravans, yet not a man molested my followers or baggage, though straggling and without guards; yet just in their rear they robbed a caravan coming from the Westward. On the 12th* I moved to Tukkia, and the next day, at the distance of six cose, Captain Scott, sent by my brother, dear as life, Ameer ul Momālic, Mr. Hastings, and Rajah Gobin Ram, on the part of my brother the Vizier ul Momālic, had the honour of paying their respects on the road. The former presented three elephants, with an ambāree sayedâr †, and a silver howdah, and a standard and flags, according to the royal ceremonial, from the governor, with addresses from him and the Nabob Vizier, expressive of their loyalty and attachment. As the Vizier had pitched tents near Almass Gunge ‡ for my reception, I halted there for the day, and the next morning encamped near the town of Mahawn ||, where letters came

* 3d May.

† A covered seat or canopy on an elephant.

‡ About 24 miles from the city of Lucnow.

|| Ten miles from the city.

from

from my dear brothers, requeſting me to halt, that they might come to wait upon me in the morning. I complied with their requeſt, and the next day, upon intelligence of their approach, ſent Mukkurrim-u'Dowlah, Syed Akber Ally Khawn, to meet and conduct them to me. At about four ghurries of the day they arrived in the preſence, when the Vizier and Governor, and alſo all the Engliſh gentlemen with them, preſented nuzzirs according to their ranks. The Vizier laid before me a peſhcuſh * of four elephants, with a ſilver ambarree, five horſes, and a ſtandard of drums. I honoured each of my brothers with a khelâat of a turban, a goſhebund †, and jeggah and ſerpeiſk ‡ of jewels, with a neem-aſteen, a ſtring of pearls, a ſhield and ſword, alſo an elephant and horſe. After ſome ghurries I diſmiſſed them with the favours of the Betel and Otter. On the 17th I marched to the Bowley, about a coſe from Lucnow, at-

* Offerings to the royal line are ſo called.

† A band of embroidery tied round the head.

‡ Jewels tied to the turban; the firſt in the form of a feather, the other fixed horizontally.

tended by the Vizier in the Khawafs, who on my alighting returned to the city. On the 18th * the Vizier and the Governor coming to meet me, conducted me to Lucnow in great pomp, and the inhabitants were filled with fuch joy and fatisfaction at my arrival, that they adorned the ftreets and fhops to exprefs their gladnefs. The Vizier, having conducted me to his own palace, performed the neceffary ceremonials of refpect, and having offered a pefhcufh of two elephants, two horfes, and a filver pallekee, together with trays of jewels, cloths, and arms, attended me to the houfe prepared for my reception in the Englifh cantonments.

* 8th May.

End of Prince Jehândâr Shâh's Narrative.

For GENTLEMEN *going to* INDIA.

BOOKS printed for J. MURRAY, No. 32, FLEET-STREET, LONDON,

And recommended by the Honourable the Court of Directors to their Governors, Councils, and other Servants abroad.

This Day is published,

Very handsomely printed at the Clarendon Press, Oxford, in Two large Volumes in Folio, Price Ten Guineas, bound;

A DICTIONARY; Persian, Arabic, and English; and English, Persian, and Arabic.

By JOHN RICHARDSON, Esq; F. S. A.

Of the Middle Temple, and of Wadham College, Oxford.

Where may be had,

1. A DISSERTATION on the Languages, Literature, and Manners of Eastern Nations. Second Edition, in One large Volume Octavo, Price 7s. bound. By the same.

2. A SPECIMEN of Persian Poetry, or Odes of Hafez, with an English Translation and Paraphrase. 4to. 5s. 3d. boards. By the same.

3. A GRAMMAR of the Arabic Language. 4to. Price 13s. bound. By the same.

4. A GRAMMAR of the Persian Language. By Sir William Jones. 4to. Price 13s. bound.

5. POEMS; consisting chiefly of Translations from the Asiatic Languages. By the same. 8vo. 6s. bound,

6. A CODE of Gentoo Laws; or Ordinations of the Pundits, from a Persian Translation; made from the Original, written in the Shanscript Language. 8vo. 7s. 6d. bound,

7. INSTITUTES of TIMOUR, improperly called Tamerlane, tranſlated from the Perſian by Major Davy and Mr. White, with Notes and Cuts, Perſian and Engliſh. 4to. 1l. 11s. 6d. boards.

8. BONTIUS's Account of the Diſeaſes which prevail in the Eaſt Indies. 8vo. 5s. bound.

9. DR. LIND's Eſſay on Diſeaſes incident to Europeans in Hot Climates. 8vo. 6s. bound.

10. DR. BLANE's Obſervations on the Diſeaſes incident to Seamen. Juſt publiſhed, large 8vo. 7s. bound.

11. CAMPBELL's Lives of the Britiſh Admirals, with plates, brought down to 1779. Four vols. large 8vo. Price 1l. 8s. bound.

12. The ENGLISH REVIEW for September 1786 (a periodical Work, which unites the State of Politics with that of Literature) and all the preceding Numbers, 1s. each.

13. The POLITICAL MAGAZINE, and Parliamentary, Naval, and Military Journal, for October, 1786, and all the preceding Numbers, 1s. each.

14 MILLAR's ORIGIN OF RANKS in Society. 8vo. 6s. bound.

15. THE MAN OF THE MOON, or Travels into the Lunar Regions, by the Man of the People. 2 vols. 6s. bound.

16. STUART's VIEW of SOCIETY in Europe, in its Progreſs from Rudeneſs to Refinement. 4to. 15s. boards.

*** At No. 32, Fleet-ſtreet, Gentlemen going to India may be ſupplied with a proper Aſſortment of valuable Books and new Publications, adapted to the Country and the Voyage